Thomas Kirwan

**Soldiering in North Carolina**

Thomas Kirwan

**Soldiering in North Carolina**

ISBN/EAN: 9783337283117

Printed in Europe, USA, Canada, Australia, Japan

Cover: Foto ©Andreas Hilbeck / pixelio.de

More available books at **www.hansebooks.com**

# SOLDIERING

— IN —

# NORTH CAROLINA;

— BEING —

THE EXPERIENCES OF A 'TYPO' IN THE PINES, SWAMPS, FIELDS, SANDY ROADS, TOWNS, CITIES, AND AMONG THE FLEAS, WOOD-TICKS, 'GRAY-BACKS,' MOSQUITOES, BLUE-TAIL FLIES, MOCCASIN SNAKES, LIZARDS, SCORPIONS, REBELS, AND OTHER REPTILES, PESTS AND VERMIN OF THE 'OLD NORTH STATE.'

EMBRACING AN ACCOUNT OF THE THREE-YEARS AND NINE-MONTHS MASSACHUSETTS REGIMENTS IN THE DEPARTMENT, THE FREEDMEN ETC., ETC., ETC.

BY "ONE OF THE SEVENTEENTH."

---

ILLUSTRATED.

---

BOSTON:
PRINTED AND PUBLISHED BY THOMAS KIRWAN.
1864.

# PREFACE.

The contents of the following pages are presented to the public as matters of fact. They embody some of the writer's experiences while serving his country in the "land of cotton." It is true his experiences are tame and unromantic when compared with those of some of the men of the Potomac or the Cumberland; but they are the best he can offer, and need no apology, as the style does, which is rough and unpolished.

Besides giving an account of the 17th Mass. Reg't, and its participation in the engagements at Kinston, Whitehall, and Goldsboro, something is said of the other old regiments in the department, and the nine months' men,—also, an account of the contrabands, their habits and disposition—anecdotes, &c.

## DEDICATION.

To the officers and men of the Seventeenth Massachusetts
Regiment, who, through no fault of their's, have only
lacked the opportunities to render their organization as famous as that of any regiment from
the old Bay State : whose services have
been mostly of that passive character
—upon the outpost picket, and
performing arduous duty in
the midst of a malarial
country—that suffers
and endures much
without exciting
comment or adding
to the laurels, of which
every true soldier is so proud :

THIS HUMBLE WORK IS DEDICATED,

By one who, with them, has braved the " pestilence that walk-
eth abroad at noonday," the fatigues of the march,
and the dangers of the battle.

# PART 1.

ENLISTMENT — DEPARTURE — THE VOYAGE — HATTERAS — UP THE NEUSE — NEWBERN — AN ACCOUNT OF THE 17TH — ON PICKET — DOING PROVOST DUTY IN NEWBERN, ETC.

It has been said that man is essentially a "fighting animal,"— that in this "world's broad field of battle" his life, from the cradle to the grave, is one continued struggle against want and its attendant circumstances, — and that he is the greatest who, be his position what it may, acts well his part. If this be true — and I think it is — then the man who goes to the war only exchanges one mode of strife for another — "the whips and scorns of time," for interminable drilling, "hard tack and salt horse,"—"the oppressor's wrong," for the hardships of the march and the dangers of the battle, — "the proud man's contumely," for the murmurings at home that he does not "clean out" the rebels in a week or two, — "the law's delay," for the tedium of garrison and camp life, — "the insolence of office," for the rule (not always gentle or humane) of men placed over him, — and the "bare bodkin," for the sword and the bayonet. And yet — and yet —

> "Ah me! what perils do environ
> The man that meddles with cold iron!
> What plaguy mischiefs and mishaps
> Do dog him still with after claps!"

The severe checks and disasters experienced by the Union arms in the Spring camaign of 1862, culminating in the "seven days' fight" before Richmond, and the retreat of McClellan's noble but suffering and crippled army to James river, while it spread sorrow and mourning throughout the land, had the effect of awakening those in power to a full sense of the nation's peril.

When the President called for more men, thereby giving effect to the wishes of the loyal people, I was one of those who helped to swell the volume of that mighty response which echoed back from the hills and prairies, cities and villages, towns and hamlets:

"We are coming, father Abraham, three hundred thousand more!"

Like others, I had to mourn the loss of a friend, — a brave young fellow, who was killed in the second of the "seven days' fight," and determined to fill his place, if I could.

On the 4th of August, 1862, I entered my name as a "raw recruit" for Co. F, 19th Mass. Reg't, as one of the quota of the town of Malden. A friend, struck by my example, or, perhaps, being in that state of mind which needs but little to turn one way or the other, joined with me; but upon going to the office in Boston where enlistments for the 19th were "done up," we were told recruiting for it was stopped. How times have altered since then, — now, I believe, it would take a battalion to fill it. We were in a fix (at least I was, who wished to go in the 19th), but there was a remedy at hand. A recruiting officer for the 17th, who had an office in Union street, received us willingly, and after being examined and sworn in, we were packed off, with some twenty other recruits, to Camp Cameron in North Cambridge. It was late in the evening when we arrived there, and no preparation being made for us —owing, I suppose, to the constant and rapid influx of recruits, which taxed to their utmost the various departments to fit out and provide for,—we had to turn in, supperless, to a bunk of downy boards, with no covering but our thin citizens' summer clothes. I thought it was a very uncomfortable resting place at the time, but it was nothing to what I have since known in the way of sleeping accommodation. The next morning I had leisure to look around me and take a survey of the mass of human nature that there commingled for the first time. And truly it was a heterogeneous compound of representatives of nearly every race of people in Europe, and plentifully sprinkled among them was the leaven of the whole—smart, shrewd, intelligent, quick-eyed and quick-witted Americans. And such a confusing babble as prevailed I never heard before. Wrangling and swearing, drinking and eating, talking and laughing,—all combined to give me no very agreeable foretaste of what I had to expect in my new vocation. I noticed others, new, like myself, to such scenes, who seemed mentally dumfounded, or unconsciously comparing the quiet routine of the life they led at home to the new one they had assumed, and, no doubt, to the great advantage of the former and dislike for the latter. But happily for us all, being the creatures of circumstances, the pliability of our natures leads us to be quickly reconciled to our lot, whatever it may be. The change of life from a citizen to that of a soldier is so radical that few like it at first; but by degrees it becomes endurable, and finally, often, desirable. The recent re-enlistments prove this.

There were several "characters" among the recruits in camp, to whom, if I could, I would devote a few pages, as well as to management of the camp and the method of dovetailing a little *innocent* private business into that of the public, as practiced by some of the little-great men in authority there; but as paper costs 22 cents per pound, I am warned that I must leave out here and condense there, which is not so pleasant after all.

Men were arriving every day in squads of from twenty to fifty, and leaving at intervals in detachments of from 100 to 500, to be distributed among their respective regiments at the seat of war. At length our turn came. It was on a Friday. — Now, Friday, though generally considered by superstitious persons an unlucky day, has often proved a lucky one for me. I was born on Friday; was married on Friday; and now I started to go to the war on Friday. I shouldn't wonder if on some Friday in the future I would die—and that will be another great event in my life. Well, we started on a Friday afternoon, and taking the cars at the Old Colony depot in Boston and the boat at Fall River, found ourselves next morning in the city of New York. We were quartered in barracks on White street, furnished with filthy beds, miserable "grub," and allowed free range of the city. A lieutenant (from Haverhill, I believe) had charge of our squad, which numbered about a hundred, and some of his enthusiastic admirers in the crowd presented him with a sword. There was, of course, a presentation speech, enthusiastic, pathetic, patriotic and warlike, and a response suitable and sentimental. It made a good impression on me at the time; but then I had yet to learn the difference between what an Indian would call "talk fight" and "fightem."

On the following Monday afternoon, with all "traps" snugly bestowed and knapsacks strapped on, we were drawn up in front of the barracks, when the lieutenant stepped out in front and proposed three cheers for the barrack-master, which were given; but I did not join in, even in dumb show, having too much consientiousness to outrage the finer feelings of my stomach by cheering for an individual who had cheated and abused it. We then took up our line of march for the transport, and went along almost unnoticed save by a few patriotic individuals who bade us a fervent God-speed and wished that good-fortune might attend us wherever we went; but the great mass seemed hardened to the sight of their fellow men going away from amongst them to explore unknown fields of danger, and to purchase with their life's blood a continuance and perpetuity of that nationality which has made the United States of America the first among nations. As these thoughts entered my mind, they suggested the picture of the hundreds of thousands of devoted men who passed through this great city, with all their hardest and most bitter experiences—hardships and dangers, sickness and death —before them, many, very many of them to return again no more; and I began to realize that, though still in a land of peace and plenty, a few days would bring me out upon far different scenes and into circumstances that would require a bold heart to meet as they ought to be met. Luckily for us all, the future cannot be penetrated, or we should be mourning calamities before they befall us; dreading dangers before they threaten, and finally become unmanned at the awful prospect impending over our future. Still there is in the expectancy of danger something that is fascinating, and something, too, that even while we dread we seek; and this feeling, the result of a strange curiosity, enlivened by hope and the love of excitement, is what often keeps up the spirit of the soldier and urges him on, even when worn out with fatigue and well-nigh exhausted, to renewed energy and more determined acts of bravery.

The transport we embarked upon was a dilapidated steamer called the "Haze" (who that ever took passage in her to or from Dixie can forget the old tub?), a miserably appointed vessel, whose officers and crew seemed better fitted for the penitentiary than for the station they held. It was in this vessel that I first learnt some of the hardships and inconveniences of a soldier's life. Just before the hawser was cast off, an Irish apple-woman came on board, her basket well laden with fruit, and said—"Come, me poor boys; it's not many of these ye'll get in the place ye're goin' to—so help yerselves! 'Tis all I have to give ye, except me blessin'—and may God bless ye all, and bring ye safe back agin to the frinds ye have at home!"

She then proceeded to distribute the apples (and fine ones they were) to the boys, many of whom, thinking more of the apples than the blessing, rushed eagerly in saying, "bully for you, old lady!" nearly overturning her in their desire to possess as much of the fruit as possible. As for me, I was content to let them have the fruit—the blessing and good wishes of the warm-hearted old woman was all-sufficient for my desires. She stepped ashore, and as she disappeared in the crowd on the pier, I heard one of the lucky ones, who was luxuriating in the fruits of his scramble, remark to another lucky one,—"D——d good apples!—that's a bully old woman,—how did you like her malediction?" "Big thing," was the response.

The hawser was finally cast off, and, backing slowly out of the dock, the steamer was soon under full headway down the bay. What my emotions were as I gazed (perhaps) for the last time upon the surrounding scenes, I will not tire the reader by giving expression to,—doubtless they resembled in a manner those of thousands of others who had gone the same road before me. My comrades, however, as a general thing, were merry, and talked of the promised land (Dixie) in a tone that showed how high their hopes ran; but presently, as we passed Sandy Hook, and the regular and continuous swell of the ocean set in, many who were before lively as kittens became tame and wretched-looking enough. It was dark before we passed the Highlands, and, though we could not see the Jersey shore we heard of it from the breakers, here and there catching glimpses of lights which told us that even among its barren sands many had found homes. But let Jersey pass, and Delaware, and Virginia's eastern shore — "away, away down South in Dixie" we go. But how few, comparatively, of our detachment were now so eager, after encountering one enemy, to meet another? And yet, I verily believe, many of these poor fellows would prefer at that time to run their chances in battle (if only on the land) than be tossed about at the mercy of the waves and so thoroughly sea-sick. As for me, whose somewhat eventful life had often before sent me "down to the sea in ships," I had no feelings of nausea, and consequently enjoyed the surroundings, the fresh, bracing sea air seeming to instil new vigor into my frame, which twenty years of toil in a printing office (with short intermissions) had tended to impair. Thus situated I could look about me, and I observed some who were formerly the jolliest of our band now the saddest and most forlorn. One in particular (a fine young fellow, whom we dubbed "the colonel") who had been the life of our party, now, pale and sad, with not a word to say, lay doubled up inside the coils of a hawser, as forlorn as the Wandering Jew (by Eugene Sue). It was no more, with him, "Away daown Saouth in a few days—hooray!" We passed the Chesapeake, (Fortress Monroe,) Cape Henry and the dismal coast beyond, and on the third evening neared land to the north of Cape Hatteras.—But such land! A long, low bar of sand, stretching away as far as the eye could reach, relieved at intervals by huge hummocks covered with a stunted growth of trees, whose ragged and forlorn limbs and inclined position made them appear as if a fierce hurricane all the while tore through their branches, threatening to uproot and cast them away forever. "There," said I to the 'colonel,' who had come upon deck when he heard we were near Hatteras, and stood beside me grasping the rail,—"There is Dixie, my jolly 'colonel.' We have come 'away daown Saouth in a few days,' haven't we; and how do you like the lay of the land? What—can't you even say 'hooray?'" But only a faint smile was the answer. Shortly after dark we descried Hatteras light, which we neared about ten o'clock; but the captain would not venture in, and so we had to lay "off and on" till daylight, which was no pleasant job, for "the wind rose and the rain fell," and gave those who selected the deck for their sleeping place (myself among the number), with the assistance of an occasional dash of salt water, a pretty thorough soaking. As soon as it was clear day our craft headed for the "swash," the wind blowing a small gale, the rain coming in squalls as if some fretful genius presided over this unhappy coast, and the waves running in shore like race-horses, spreading their foam in a thin gray mist over the narrow line of sand, which seemed endeavoring almost in vain to keep its back above the water. To our right, and north of the inlet, were the forts taken by Gen. Butler in his first Coast Expedition. Only one of these, Fort Hatteras, is now used. The other has either sunk into the sand or been almost wholly destroyed by the action of the waves. Fort Hatteras is an earthwork, but so admirably situated as to prove an almost impassible barrier to anything but ironclads. Beyond and around the fort on the land or sand side, were a few buildings used for quarters for the garrison and for ordnance stores. Anchored in the Sound, near by, were supply ships, transports, and old hulks; while here and there rows of disconsolate timbers, lifting their dripping heads above the tide, told the fate of many a noble ship of the glorious Expedition of Gen. Burnside. We "hove to" after entering the Sound to deliver the mails for the Fort; and the change from the violent rolling, tossing and pitching was such as to inspire even my old friend the 'colonel' with something of the spirit he was wont to display ere old Neptune changed his tune. After taking a look at the Fort and its surroundings, I turned my eyes to the opposite shore of the inlet, when lo, there stretched out in an almost straight line from the point into the Sound a troop or flock of—what? That was the puzzle to my mind. Were they huge gulls or windbags, cormorants or cranes, devils or dogfish? Fowl, flesh, or fish? I watched them with close attention while asking myself these questions; but ere my cogitations were finished they separated, spread their wings and took flight, apparently, but it seemed strange they did not rise from the surface of the water. They neared us presently, and I made them out to be, instead of birds, small sail-boats. "Love launched a fairy boat," &c. No love for us there, I guess, was my mental comment. "Pilots," I heard some one say. They came fluking towards us, their comparatively large sprit-sails hurrying them along at no contemptible rate of speed. There were about fifteen of them, and it seemed evident all could not get a job from our hazy skipper. "That's Jeff.'s navy," remarked one.

"Hooray for the boat that's ahead!" sang out the 'colonel.'

"Bully for the little fellow with the big sail!" exclaimed another.

"I'll bet on the cross-gaffed, giraffe-colored one!"

"Bully for the rip-staving roarer that wins!"

"Aint she a-ripping up the old salt water canvas, skearing the sharks and astonishing the sea sarpints?"

"I'll bet Jeff.'s in that boat, and he's coming to ask us to dine with him in Richmond!"

"Beauregard's in the second one!"

"No, *sir*, that's Stonewall Jackson!"

"D——n Stonewall Jackson, or any other man!" and remarks of a like character attested the interest felt in this novel contest by others as well as myself. The boats were pelting away in fine style, each having a loose rein. Then hurrah, my hearties! the lucky man wins, and "first come first served!" Two of the number were distinctly ahead of all the rest, and one of these slightly ahead of the other.

"But Cutty Sark, before the rest,
Hard upon noble Maggie prest—"

so that when they came up it was difficult to say which was first, and both came aboard to dispute the point, while the remaining unsuccessful ones kept on, as if philosophically resigned to a fate they could not overcome. Our hazy skipper, who was not very particular about expenses when Uncle Sam had to foot the bills, and to end all disputes, took both pilots—a piece of diplomacy I hardly expected his thick head capable of conceiving. The anchor was hoisted, and away we sped over the dark, swampy waters of Pamlico Sound. Roanoke Island lay to our right, and ever and anon we caught glimpses of the low, swampy lands of Hyde and Plymouth counties. To the left or south we beheld a continuation of islands, and shortly after the main land of Cartaret county became visible. It seemed almost wholly unsettled, the wilderness appearance being only here and there relieved by the small clearing of a turpentine plantation, fishing establishment, or the twenty-acre field of a "poor white."

We soon made Neuse river—a noble stream, upon the banks of which turpentine, pitch, rosin and tar enough might be made to supply the markets of the North. As we ascended the river the signs of habitation became more numerous although seeming "few and far between" to the eye accustomed to the more frequent settlements on Northern rivers, and the sombre hues of the pine, cedar and cypress forests were occasionally enlivened by the brighter foliage of persimmon, walnut and fig trees, the last flourishing here in great luxuriance, bearing two or rather a continuation of crops of delicious fruit in a season, and may be seen on every farm or plantation in patches of from a few trees to orchards of twenty-five acres in extent. We could also trace the courses of the many "branches" or creeks from the lighter foliage of the gum and other water-loving trees.

In the afternoon we passed Slocum's Creek, where Burnside landed his troops the evening before the battle of Newbern, and soon the spires of this city, and the shipping, hove in sight; and towards the close of the day, after a sail of ten hours, during which time we steamed eighty or ninety miles, we drew up at the pier and prepared to disembark, thankful that we could again set foot on land and leave forever the accursed "Haze" and her brutal captain and crew.

"Mind, I tell you," said one of the latter, "bad as you think the old 'Haze' is, you will before long be glad to be on board of her again—if you'd be *let !*"

He was laughed at; but I doubt not many of them, ere six months elapsed, wished themselves anywhere else than where they were. Still they could not see it then, but felt happy, like young bears, with all their troubles before them.

The dilapidated and seedy condition of the wharves, and the ruins of houses, mills and turpentine factories, impressed me with a premonition of what I should yet witness of the ravages of war in this fair land.

The city of Newbern bears the appearance of some age, is regularly laid out, the streets intersecting each other at right angles, and well protected from the merciless heat of summer by fine old elm trees, intermixed here and there with the chaney and other trees the names of which I do not recollect. The city is located at a point of land formed by the junction of the Trent river with the Neuse, and has altogether an imposing appearance viewed from the approach by water.

The Mass. 23d Reg't, Col. Kurtz, (who was provost marshal,) was then doing provost duty in the city.

When the order for landing was given, each scrambled ashore with the whole of his household furniture upon his back. After passing through a part of the city, we struck the railroad bridge, (destroyed by the rebels after their defeat, but rebuilt by our forces,) crossing which, and marching a mile or two, halted at the encampment of the 17th on the Trent river, where we were welcomed by the men of the various companies, many of whom found friends and acquaintances among the 'raw recruits.' My comrade had friends in the Malden Company (K), of which we were henceforth to form a part, and we received a hearty welcome from the members of mess 5, some of the good-natured ones of which taxed themselves to the amount of nearly a dollar to procure from the sutler something more palatable for our first meal than 'hard tack and salt horse.'

After 'taps' the lights were put out, and we disposed ourselves upon the tent-floor to sleep, in the manner of spokes of a cartwheel, our feet toward the hub, which consisted of the gun-rack around the tent-pole, there to revolve in the circle of dreams of home and friends far distant. Before closing our eyes, however, and while inquiries were plied and answered thick and fast, one of the mess startled the newcomers by exclaiming—

"A rat! A rat! I have him!"

"Pass him around!" was the general cry.

"Now I've got him!" another exclaimed. This was followed by a gurgling noise, as in the first instance.

The 'rat' came nearer, and presently I smelt him. There was no mistaking that 'rat,'—he came from Jersey and was surnamed 'lightning,' and cost the fourth part of a soldier's pay for one month. Being eagerly pressed to taste him, I did *taste*, but that was all—the smell was enough, and I passed him over to the next man.

Sleep at length overcome me, and I dreamed of rats made of glass, squealing "Jersey lightning! Jersey lightning!" until morning, when I awoke to find myself surrounded by comrades busy eating breakfast. Beside me stood a dipper of smoking hot coffee, some hard bread and salt beef, provided by one of the most thoughtful of my new friends.

After guard-mounting (9 A.M.) the recruits were drawn up in line, assigned to the various companies, examined by the surgeon, and, after a few words of encouragement or advice from their captains (and mayhap a glass of whisky), returned to their quarters, feeling relieved, no doubt, that the affair was over.

Thus, in the course of about an hour, the recruits were disposed of, and duly incorporated with the regiment—to share in its messes and marches, its skirmishes and scratches, its picket duty and plunder, its whisky and quinine, its tents and hospitals, its hard tack and salt horse, its pea soup and pea coffee, its baked beans without brown bread, its pride and its perils, its glory and its graveyards.

The following is a list of the principal staff and line officers of the 17th, the companies and where they were raised, together with an account—taken from a diary or journal of Mr. Wm. Noble, of Saugus, (the first color sergeant)—of the doings of the regiment from its inception down to the 5th of January, 1862:

*Colonel*—THOMAS I. C. AMORY.

[Mr. Amory was born in Boston, Nov. 27, 1828; entered West Point in 1846, and graduated in 1851, when he was appointed 2d lieutenant in the 7th Infantry, ordered to Fort Smith in Arkansas, and was promoted 1st lieutenant in 1855. In 1858 he was ordered to Utah, under the command of the late Gen. Albert Sidney Johnson, who joined the rebels at the outbreak of the Southern rebellion and was killed at Shiloh; was ordered to Boston on recruiting service in 1860, and was promoted to a captaincy May 7, 1861. When the war broke out, he obtained leave of absence from the War Department, and accepted a commission from Gov. Andrew as Colonel of the 17th Mass. Vols., on Sept. 7th, 1861. Since the regiment has been in the Department of North Carolina, he has acted as General of Brigade; but whether his nomination for the brigadiership has been confirmed or not, I am unable to say. Of this I am certain, however, that there are few officers at this time serving in our armies better capable of wearing the star or more fully deserving of it than Thomas I. C. Amory.]

*Lieut. Colonel*—JOHN F. FELLOWS.

[Mr. Fellows, of Chelsea, is well known in Boston, having been for many years connected with its daily press. He was also an active member of the State Militia. When the war broke out he offered his services to Gov. Andrew, from whom he received a commission as Lieut. Colonel of the 17th Reg't on the 21st of August, 1861. He has proved himself a capable officer and a thoroughly brave man. I shall have frequent occasion to speak of him hereafter.]

*Major*—JONES FRANKLE. (Now, LUTHER DAY.)

[Mr. Frankle is a Prussian by birth, and served in the war of 1848 in Germany, at which time he did not "fight mit Sigel," but against him. He received his commission as Major of the 17th on the 1st of August, 1861; and proved himself a capable and efficient officer. In June, 1863, he resigned his commission in the 17th for the purpose of raising an artillery regiment (the 2d Mass. Heavy Artillery) which he now commands, and which is doing duty in the field and in forts in the various parts of North Carolina held by our forces. He was succeeded by senior captain (Co. F) Luther Day, of Haverhill, a very good officer.]

*Adjutant*—B. N. MANN. (Now, H. A. CHEEVER.)

[Mr. Mann was, I believe, for many years connected with the Boston Post Office. He is a brave man, and generous as he is brave. He was succeeded by Mr. Cheever in the Fall of '62.]

*Quartermaster*—Capt. HARRIS was commissioned Quartermaster of the 17th; but resigned in the Fall of '61, and was succeeded by Lieut. (afterwards Capt.) THOMPSON, who died at Newbern in October, '62. Lieut. DEXTER succeeded, and is the present incumbent.

*Surgeon*—ISAAC F. GALLOUPE.

[Dr. Galloupe is a hard-working, skillful, efficient and humane man, and discharges his duty in a manner that commands the respect and gratitude of every man who comes under his treatment. The Dr. is from Lynn.]

*Assistant Surgeon*—WM. H. W. HINDS, of Boston.

[The men have no exalted opinion of this Dr.'s kindness or capacity, though he seems attentive and a hard worker. Perhaps his unpopularity arises from the fact that he unmercifully doses all whom he considers 'bummers' (i. e., those who are too lazy to do duty and 'play sick' to escape its performance) with salts, jalap, blue pills, and especially quinine; but I think he often punishes in this manner the deserving as well as the guilty.]

Co. *A*—Capt. Henry Splaine, of Haverhill—was raised principally in Newburyport.

Co. *B*—Capt. Enoch F. Tompkins, of Haverhill (vice Capt. S. C. Bancroft, S. Danvers, resigned)—South Danvers.

Co. *C*—Capt. Nehemiah P. Fuller—Danvers.

Co. *D*—Capt. Ivory N. Richardson, of Malden (Capt. Levi Thompson, of Cambridge, deceased)—Salisbury and Amesbury.

Co. *E*—Capt. Michael McNamara, of Haverhill—Stoneham and Haverhill.

Co. *F*—Capt. Day (now Major)—Haverhill.

Co. *G*—Capt. G. W. Kenney, of Danvers—Rockport and Salem.

Co. *H*—Capt. J. K. Lloyd—Boston and Fall River.

Co. *I*—Capt. Wm. W. Smith, of Danvers (vice Capt. Thos. Weir)—Lawrence.

Co. *K* — Capt. Joseph R. Simonds, of Melrose—Malden, Medford and Saugus.

---

"Recruiting for this regiment commenced as early as the fall of Fort Sumter, but owing to the embarrassed condition of the State, the hesitation of the General Government in regard to accepting troops, and the want of authority on the part of the Governor to act, this regiment was obliged to wait from week to week without any decisive answer as to the intention of the Government, concerning its organization. The companies were formed on the militia basis, and were desirous of a regimental organization, and to be mustered into the service, but every effort which the company officers made in that direction, seemed to be counteracted by the dominant political and monied influence which was brought to bear in favor of other regimental organizations, to the disparagement and detriment of the companies comprising the 17th. While others were splendidly provided for by private munificence, and hurried off to the seat of war, this regiment was unprovided by the State with an organization, clothing, arms, equipments or rations. An opinion prevailed at one time, that all idea of a regimental organization must be given up, and the companies enter the United States service, through some other State organization. Captains Fuller of Danvers, and Day of Haverhill, determined on bringing the matter to a focus.

"They visited the Governor, and after several ineffectual efforts to get an audience, at length succeeded, and informed His Excellency that they were going into the army, and should take their commands with them; that they wanted to go in a Massachusetts Regiment, and unless accepted by the State, should go into the Mozart Regiment of New York, as one or two other companies from Massachusetts had already done. Orders were given them by the Governor to go into the camp at Lynnfield. The other companies of which this regiment is composed, were ordered to the same place, and all arrived there between the 10th and 12th of July. They were mustered into the United States service on the 22d, remained in camp until the 23d of August, when they were ordered to Baltimore, and arrived in that city on the 25th, at 4 o'clock P.M. The principal duty of the regiment thus far, had been of a police character, and it was moved about either as a whole or a part, from one portion of the city to another, as circumstances required.

"Nov. 15, Co.'s F, K, E, G, H, and C, with Captain Nims' Battery, were detailed to form a part of the brigade under command of General Lockwood, for an expedition into the counties of Accomac and Northampton, Va., for the purpose of breaking up a rebel force concentrating there. The expedition went on board a steam transport, and on the 17th arrived at Newtown. Here they pitched their tents for the night, and the next day marched a distance of sixteen miles into the country. The rebels had felled trees across the roads in many places to ob-struck the advance of the troops, but they were cleared away with but little delay. One deserted rebel battery pierced for four guns, was found on this day's march.

"On the 19th, the regiment reached Oak Hall, and on the 20th the men went out fowling, and were very successful, taking a large amount of game, which was dressed and partaken of by the men with double relish, as they were on short rations of hard bread and salt junk, and were much exhausted by the fatigues of their march. On the 21st marched to Drummondtown, a distance of twenty-seven miles, performing the journey in eight hours, notwithstanding the many obstructions thrown across the road by the rebels, and the burned bridges which required them to march round, following the bend of the streams. On this march, between Oak Hall and Drummondtown, another rebel battery was discovered, pierced for fourteen guns. The stars and stripes were at once raised over it, and three rousing cheers given.

"November 23, took from the rebels seven guns, 150 small arms, one barrel of powder, besides some swords, shot and shell. At the jail were stored 8,000 rounds of cartridges and 200 small arms, which were also taken. Two gun-carriages and one brass howitzer were also found secreted in the woods, and captured. On the 26th, marched to Pongoteague, a distance of twelve miles, and found another deserted battery.

"November 27th, marched from Pongoteague to Franktown, a distance of twelve miles; and on the 28th, marched to Eastville, thirteen miles, taking on the way one brass cannon, seven horses, some small arms and swords, besides several other articles contraband of war. The rebels had an unfinished earthwork here which they deserted on the approach of the Federal troops.

"A very large proportion of the arms and military stores captured were returned by Gen. Lockwood to the parties claiming them, creating great dissatisfaction among the troops, and rendering the General liable to the suspicion that he sympathized with the rebels.

"The object of the expedition having been attained, the brigade was broken up, and the Mass. 17th embarked at Cherrystone on the 1st and 2d of Dec., and sailed on the 4th for Baltimore, where they arrived the same evening, and went into their old quarters. On the 18th they commenced building barracks [on Stewart's Place] for winter quarters and moved into them on the 5th of January." (These barracks are still standing, and used as a general hospital.)

In February Co.'s F and H relieved the 6th Michigan at McKim's Place, and K and G the 4th Wisconsin at Patterson's Park, those regt's being destined to form part of Gen. Butler's force then about to sail for New Orleans. On the 14th of March four other Co.'s of the 17th were ordered to Fort Marshall, East Baltimore, to assist in defending that fortification from an attack by rebel sympathizers, who, emboldened by the destructive raid of the Merrimac in Hampton Roads, meditated a rising in Baltimore, if not throughout the State.

When the 17th arrived in Baltimore they found the people of that city nearly all 'secesh' in sentiment, and seeming only constrained from rising by the presence in, and passage through, the city, of large numbers of troops. It will then be readily inferred that the men of this regiment had no very enviable task to perform in endeavoring to keep the peace and making these disaffected people see the evil of their ways. In doing this, however, they were not fools enough to use moral suasion alone—that would be casting pearls before swine—No; they used arguments that were far more convincing, such as street drills, practicing at street firing, &c., all of which turned the hate of the 'secesh' citizens into fear—and, finally, their fear became a feeling of respect. What if the men were insulted every time they walked the streets—the women (who were the most outspoken) at length became weary of abusing them, and the men who attempted to insult them never tried that game a second time; for they found in the men of this regiment a spirit that would brook no abuse—an indomitable, dare-devil disposition that met them half way with a bowie knife as long and as keen as their own, and a pistol as deadly. Thus they fought their way to respect, and this latter feeling ripened into affection, which is shown by the fact that when the regiment was about to sail for North Carolina, the ladies of Baltimore presented it with a magnificent silk flag, upon which was painted a fine portrait of Washington.

On the 27th of March, '62, the regiment embarked at Baltimore for Newbern, North Carolina, which place they reached on the 1st of April, and encamped on a field to the west of the city,—near where Fort Totten now stands, and which was then in process of construction. On the 7th of April the regiment was ordered out on picket duty—the left wing to Jackson's place on the Trent road, and the right wing to a place called the Red House on the Neuse road, relieving the 24th and 27th Mass. regt's. The regiment remained on picket until the 30th May, during which time they had frequent skirmishes with the enemy, and made several raids and forays into the enemy's country. Shortly after the regiment went to Jackson's place, a few companies made a dash about nine miles up the Trent road to a church, where they had a smart brush with the 'rebs,' two of whom were killed and one wounded, and one taken prisoner. It was here that one of those ludicrous incidents occurred which often serve to relieve the dark outline of war's grim visage. When the enemy were come up with, and firing became frequent, Lt. Col. Fellows ordered the men to open right and left to let the artillery pass to the front. One of the captains, mistaking the full purport of the order, and thinking the ranks were to be opened to allow the rebels a fair field and an open road to come into close quarters with his men, sang out:

"Open right and left, and let the d—d scallywags through!"

Captain Weir, of Co. I, with his command, and as many volunteers as wished to accompany them, made a raid to Pollockville to capture cotton, and anything else that might prove of value to the "rebs" in their belligerent character. Now, as this was not the first time Tom Weir (as he was familiarly called) had invaded the sanctity of that village, the rebs had a special eye to his movements, and lay in wait for him.

He had a mule team loaded with cotton, corn and other plunder preceding him on his return, which the rebs in ambush allowed to pass; but just as the company got opposite to where they were concealed, they poured in a volley which killed three and wounded the same number—and put the men into such a panic that they fled. The captain stood, and endeavored to rally them, but to no purpose, and he had to follow and leave those who had fallen to their fate (which was being stripped of arms, equipments, clothes, and whatever valuables they had upon them), until rescued by the reinforcement which came up promptly—to find the rebels flown. For this Captain Weir was court-martialed, and dismissed the service—a sentence which was universally condemned by the men, who considered him a brave officer, having done all a man could do under the circumstances.

Captain Lloyd of Company H, next tried his hand in Pollocksville, but lost three men by the upsetting of a boat in the Trent river on his outward march. He, however, took some plunder and two prisoners.

The results of all these scouts and forays were the capture of several thousand dollars' worth of cotton, corn, cattle, hens, &c., (there must have been *foul* play somewhere).

The regiment returned to Newbern on the 30th of May,

and on the 26th of June were ordered to Swift Creek—upon approaching the bridge leading across which they were fired upon by the rebels (without sustaining any damage) who had a battery masked by a breastwork or fort of shingles. The 17th charged across the bridge in fine style (the bridge was a lightly built one, and swayed and shook under the combined weight of 600 men in such a manner as to lead to the belief that it would break down, but it didn't) ; but upon crossing they found the enemy had flown. Three companies went up the road in pursuit some distance, but the 'rebs' were nowhere to be found. They halted near a dwelling house, when some of the men went into an adjoining negro hut, where a pot of meat and cabbage was in process of being cooked, which they proceeded to confiscate ; but just as they had commenced their feast an officer came up and drove them off, saying :

"Dum thee, did thee coom here to ploonder."

At the same time, it was asserted, though I don't believe it, that the officer who thus drove them from the feast had his pockets filled with sweet potatoes and other " ploonder." Three prisoners were taken. One of them a lad about 16 years old, was thus interrogated by the Major :

" Vat for you be guerilla for ?"

" I'm not a guerilla, sir ; I'm in the regular Confederate service."

"Vat for you lay in ambush, den ?"

" I didn't lay in any bush, sir ; I was standing behind a tree."

" Ha ! You be von rascally guerilla, and we vill shtring you up to a tree, ven we arrive in Newbern !"

But it is needless to say this threat was not carried out.

The reg't here received orders to rejoin the division (the 9th army corps) which was about to leave the Department with Gen. Burnside, and started of a Sunday morning 28th (without breakfast) on their return. The weather was intensely hot, and the sand on the road was ankle deep. The case, however, was pressing, and the men were urged to their utmost; but the task was too much for them,—and when the reg't arrived at the landing about 4 P.M., after a march of 22 miles, it numbered little more than a full company—the remaining 400 or 500 being distributed along the road for miles back. They, however, kept coming in in squads of from two to twenty during the remaining part of the afternoon and evening—and a more tired and thoroughly used up lot of men it would be difficult to find anywhere. To make matters worse, when the reg't arrived at the landing opposite Newbern, they found no transportation for them, and nothing wherewith to satisfy the cravings of hunger. It was not until about 12 o'clock at night that they received a ration of hard bread and salt meat; but no vessels arrived to transport them across, and they were forced to lay out upon the sandy beach, without shelter, in a pelting, pitiless rain, which had set in early in the evening. Next morning a couple of scows or flat-boats arrived, and they were taken across; but Gen. Burnside pitying their forlorn and used up condition, and thinking it would be an act of cruelty to put men in such a state on board transports, ordered the 6th New Hampshire reg't to take their place. Thus the Seventeenth were cheated by fate out of their share of the glory of South Mountain, Antietam, Bull Run 2d, Fredericksburg, Chancellorsville, and Knoxville; and were compelled to silently and doggedly face and fight the most deadly of human foes in its own malarial fens and swamps.

About the first of July the reg't was ordered to camp on the south side of the Trent river near the county bridge, to do picket and outpost duty, which consisted of sending a company to Bray's Ferry and plantation about three miles out, and another to Evans' Mills—seven miles down the railroad towards Beaufort.

About July 25th the regiment went in an expedition to Pollocksville, and constructed a bridge across the Trent river for the entire column to cross upon, after reaching which place, Col. Amory, who was in command, decided to push on to Trenton; but upon approaching to within four miles of the latter place he found the enemy too strong, and withdrew without bringing on an engagement.

August 20th, six companies of the 17th went to Swift Creek, again, accompanied by a section of the New York Marine Artillery and four boat howitzers. Lt. Col. Fellows, who was in command of the expedition, having missed the boat that conveyed the reg't and artillery across the river, the command devolved upon the Major, who marched them about a mile from the landing, and halted to await the Colonel's coming. The column halted opposite a dwelling, and, as is often the case under like circumstances, there was a rush for the well to fill canteens. Two of the men, however, strayed into a field and were making a flank movement upon a pile of tumble-down log outbuildings, supposed to abound in hens, chickens, eggs, &c. One of these men, a very tall and large specimen of humanity was named Gilman; the other was a small man, and, for my purpose, nameless. The vigilant Major detected this unauthorized flanking affair, and, being determined to put a stop to all such unmilitary proceedings, sung out:

"Vat for you shtray off dat way? Come back, I say to you! Dou-bel *twit!*" (quick)

The little man obeyed, and came back at a dog-trot. Gilman, however, hastened back slowly—at much too slow a gait to suit his impatient superior, who yelled out again:

"Dou-bel twit!—I say—dou-*bel* TWIT!"

But no faster came Gilman on, and the Major (who was a little man) rushed to him, and seizing him by the coat collar as he was crossing a fence, dragged him over,—then, drawing his sword and flourishing it about the head of the still doggedly defiant Gilman, exclaimed:

"You tink, because I am small, I'm be afraid of you? I will let you know! Dou-bel twit! now, or I will make two Gilman of you!"

There was a man called Tom Croke in Co. E—an extremely hard ticket—quarrelsome, venomous, and altogether thoroughly depraved. He had been a source of trouble and annoyance to the officers of the company ever since he came into it. On this expedition, I believe, he shot the top of one of his fingers off—an accident, as he told the captain (McNamara)—

"Devil d——n you," replied the latter, "it's a pity it wasn't your head!"

Tom Croke, for this or some other misdemeanor, was subsequently court-martialed and sent to Fort Macon to serve out his time, from which place he escaped to the rebels. On his way from the Fort to rebeldom he met a deserter coming into our lines, whom he directed as to the best route to pursue, and who in turn gave him such information as he desired to facilitate his escape.

When the expedition arrived at the bridge over Swift Creek it was evening. Our cavalry, which had preceded them, were bivouacked for the night on the other side, and our men at first took them to be rebels, but were soon undeceived.

There was a store-house in the village of Swift Creek, containing a variety of articles in the dry goods, grocery and merchandise line. Some of the boys smelt the plunder, and proceeded to confiscate. The wife of the owner of the store suspecting what was going on, went to Col. Fellows and told him the men were breaking in, and he immediately repaired to the scene of operations to put a stop to such work. A member of Co. K, who had been left on the watch, gave warning of the colonel's approach, and the raiders hid.

"What ho! there,—what does all this mean? What are you doing here?" (To Co. K man.)

"I'm on guard, sir."

"All right, madam," said the colonel; "you see there is a guard on."

What plunder the boys obtained it would be bootless to relate.

The expedition returned to Newbern, burning the bridge after them.

The camp of the 17th was situated in what was formerly a cotton field, on the banks of the river Trent, affording excellent facilities for washing clothes and bathing, of which most of the men availed themselves,—and at all hours of the day men could be seen bathing in the river, or squatted along its margin washing clothes. It seemed at first sight to one unacquainted with the peculiarities of the climate, to be a well chosen and healthy location (and indeed it was about the best in the vicinity); but the hanging mosses that everywhere shrouded the few solitary cedars which still survived the ravages of the pioneer's axe, showed the unmistakeable presence of fever and ague—that pest of new and warm countries. About a couple of hundred yards up the river, close to the county bridge, a fort was in process of completion,—the work of 'contrabands,' numbers of whom I observed busily employed in and around it. Beyond this were encamped some light batteries; while still further on, and at the crossing of a deep, sluggish stream called Brice's Creek, a number of detailed men were at work constructing a block-house (a square-built fort, made of hewn logs, compactly put together—and most conveniently constructed to be knocked to pieces by a six-pounder about a poor devil's ears). Between the artillery camp and the block-house was a brick dwelling-house, once the property of Gov. Speight, the late owner and family of which fled after the battle of Newbern. This house was afterwards demolished to supply bricks for chimneys of barracks built near by in the Fall. To the rear of this house, about 75 yards distant, beautifully shaded by fine old trees, was the tomb of Gen. Speight, a revolutionary hero, and one of the early Governors of North Carolina.

The plain on which the 17th were encamped is about two and a half miles long, and from one-half to two miles wide, and had, evidently, before the rude hand of war obliterated their boundaries and landmarks, consisted of two or three plantations. This plain was an excellent place for drilling, and nearly all reviews were held there.

The whole field gave evidence of having, at different times and in different parts, been camped upon by infantry, artillery, and cavalry—and everywhere evidences of military occupation were visible in the shape of broken bottles, dilapidated canteens, dippers and plates, and remnants of worn-out shoes, coats, blouses, pants, and harness, forgotten tent-stakes, sink holes and caved-in wells. While overhead and around, unnoticed and unmolested, on lazy wing sailed the huge turkey-buzzard, scenting the dead carcase and decayed garbage from afar, and patiently biding the absence of man from its vicicinity ere he descended to gorge himself therewith.

I noticed a great variety of wild flowers in the fields, some of which were very beautiful. A species of cactus grows wild here; but is a very inferior kind. Wild garlic is also to be met with everywhere. A coarse grass, called Bear's grass, grows in bunches here, the leaves of which, when subjected to a roasting process in hot ashes, are uncommonly strong, and take the place of small ropes and cords with the natives, who apply it in a variety of ways, from the suspension of a dead pig to the tying of a shoe, or temporarily supplying the place of a lost button. From the centre of these bunches of Bears grass a stem five or six feet high shoots up in the spring-time, which is crowned with a crest of yellow flowers very beautiful to behold at a distance.

A few days' experience of camp-life gave me a better knowledge of its comforts and discomforts, its tribulations and my philosophy. It was the middle of August, and the weather very warm. The first night of my abode in my new quarters was undisturbed from any cause, from the fact that I was tired after the sea-voyage. But the second night I was destined to feel some of the annoyances to be endured by campaigners in warm climates. Mosquitoes revel in this congenial atmosphere, as do also the blue-tail fly, and a species of biting insect like the common house-fly, while gallinippers, gnats, ants, and biting sand-fleas, (which play second fiddle to the old-fashioned iron-clad chaps, their bites making one squirm as if twinged by a bad conscience,) and grey-backs, all attack the hapless sleeper in succession, in a body, by detail, in squads, battalion,—in brigades drawn up in echelon—in front, flank and rear. They scale the walls of his fortress in the very teeth of a fierce cannonade of imprecations—burst the barriers of bedclothes—penetrate the abatti of woolen socks and tightly-tied drawers—and though, even after gaining the inside of your works, they are subjected to a deadly cross-fire of small arms, yet they invariably "attain the object of their reconnoisance." The bayonet is powerless against them, and they never draw off from the attack till fairly exhausted with the feast of blood.

What surprised me most was the utter indifference manifested by the veterans to the petty annoyance of vermin and insects, and the matter-of-fact way in which they overhauled their clothing and disposed of the greybacks when found.

For about a week the recruits had "fine times," as the soldiers thought, having nothing to do but "bum around," and sleep—when they could, which was mostly in the day time. The days were excessively hot, as were the nights until about 11 or 12 o'clock, when it became uncomfortably cold.

During this week of leisure, I pretty thoroughly explored the region in the vicinity of our camp, and visited Newbern on 'pass,' but found nothing special there to note, if I may except the fact that there were many really cozy and comfortable-looking dwellings, and numerous flower and fruit gardens—some of which gave evidences of former tasteful ownership, but which seemed of late to have come in for their share of the general neglect and destruction. Those of the inhabitants who still clung to their homes seemed to wear a sullen and discontented look, with some exceptions, and these were of the mercantile class, who, with the sutlers and others who follow the wake of armies, seemed to fall in for their fair proportion of the trade.

About the greatest curiosity to me was what was called the new cemetery, in the upper section or suburb of the city,—the wall enclosing which is built of shell-rock—a curious fossil concrete obtained in some part of the State—where I do not know. There are many graves, and a few tasteful tombstones. Beyond this in what has become an open field or common, are several soldiers' graveyards consecrated by the poor fellows whose bodies repose there, who for love of fatherland, left home and kindred to return no more.

My first duty on picket was at Mr. Bray's plantation. "Old Bray" the boys called him, and being on the outpost which was near his house, I determined to give the old gentleman a call. I found Mr. and Mrs. Bray at home, the former seated on the piazza reading a newspaper, and the latter squatted on the doorstep doing 'nothing in particular.' They were a lean pair, (but their *leaning* was not on our side, as I afterwards found), and had a family of five or six lean boys and girls. They certainly looked an unromantic enough realization of our ideal Southern planter and his family. Mr. Bray was apparently about 45 years of age, and his wife perhaps as old, although she seemed much older. They both looked sour and cross enough to dispense with the use of vinegar at meal-time. But they did not seem indisposed to have a chat with the Yankee 'hirelings,' and soon I was made acquainted with all their griefs—the husband commencing the relation of them, but the wife invariably winding up.

I then for the first time learnt how this benevolent planter and his amiable wife had been abused—how, first of all, notwithstanding a 'protection' from Gen. Burnside, their 'niggers' had been enticed away, all efforts to get them back proving fruitless, owing to the "abolition officers and soldiers."

"Niggers and pigs were the only things that ever paid any ways well," put in Mrs. Bray.

They had only five pigs and three 'niggers' left now, and did not know how soon they'd go off with the rest.

Some of the soldiers who had been on picket near their plantation had behaved very bad, and had stolen and destroyed much of their corn and all their water melons (melancholy to relate); and Co. K of the 17th, was the worst of the lot—and the lady wound up with the expression of a hope "that the new recruits would be more of gentlemen than the old soldiers, and not seek to injure her as they had done."

Mr. Bray then showed me his melon patch which, though evincing some traces of the recent vandal act, still bore a goodly number, which I made a note of. He also showed me a patch of cotton, in full bloom,—and after another hour of desultory conversation, I left with the impression that old Bray was a 'great man on a small scale,' but his wife was the greater of the two.

About September 1st a storm came on, accompanied by rain, which lasted that and the following day and night, giving us and our traps a thorough soaking. During all this time I did not sleep a wink. The third morning, wet, sleepless and weary, I was detailed for guard, and was put on the third relief (from 1.

to 3 P.M., and 1 to 3 A.M), and during the first two hours of my
guard was refreshed by a 'jolly' shower of rain, which came in
at my coat collar and soon filled and overflowed my boots.

When the third relief turned in for the night, I lay down
with the rest, on the wet ground, and attempted to sleep; but it
was no go—so, lighting my pipe (sole comforter at times), I left
the tent, and sat under a tree near by, and smoked the hours
away (rain or no rain) until the third relief fell in, when taking
my musket and falling in to my place, I was soon on my post,
which extended from a tree (blown over by the wind) to the
river bank, about 85 paces distant. I felt drowsy, but paced
my beat rapidly to keep awake, until tired out, I leaned against
the inclined trunk of the fallen tree to rest awhile. My brain
was in a whirl, and everything about me seemed to reel and
oscillate unsteadily. It was moonlight, but cloudy. More than
once I thought I detected myself napping, and shook myself,
and pinched my nose and ears to keep awake. My comrade,
whose beat joined mine, came up occasionally, and we exchanged
a few words. I exhorted him if he caught me napping to rouse
me. He had left me, and was near the other end of his beat,
when, on looking after him, I beheld, about ten paces from me,
as plainly as if in daylight, the form of a huge negro. He wore
a broad-brimmed hat, a linen coat blue or *dark* striped, vest,
white shirt (seemingly of cotton,) open at the neck, around
which was a colored handkerchief tied sailor fashion, the ends
hanging down loose. His pants seemed of light fabric, checked.
I could see his countenance plainly. It seemed, if anything,
smiling, though there was something peculiar in its expression,
as well as the attitude, for the figure seemed leaning its weight
on one foot, its left hand resting on the hip, and the right arm
hanging loosely by its side. The expression of the darkey was
so peculiar—jaunty, saucy—and he looked full at me, that for a
moment I was taken by surprise,—and, during that moment

made the observations just recorded—but quickly recovering, I brought my piece to 'charge,' and called out—

"Who comes there?"

But no response was deigned by my darky visitor. I challenged again, and again, with the same result, the object still retaining its position, and regarding me with the same complacent look—when my comrade, who heard my first challenge came up, and inquired what the matter was, just as I was about bringing my piece to 'present' to fire. I pointed to the object of my challenging, who still kept his ground in the same position. He laughed at what he supposed was a joke I was trying to

come on him—not being able to see anything in the spot I pointed out,—and resumed his beat. The thought then occurred to me for the first time that what I saw was not real. What then was it? I asked myself. Surely I am not troubled with that disease known as 'nigger on the brain!' And I again leaned against the trunk of the fallen tree to think the subject over, all the while keeping my eyes fixed upon the object of my thoughts, which stood the scrutiny unmoved. Now, I am not superstitious by nature, and still less so by education and experience,—and so I viewed the apparition without a particle of fear or awe, and tried to account to myself for its appearance in the most natural and rational manner. I came to the conclusion there and then, that want of rest and the stimulation of the coffee and tobacco I had been indulging in unduly excited my brain, which produced the hallucination, on the same principle that it is produced in certain stages of drunkenness, called delirium tremens. This was a very fair deduction; but still in front of me stood the grinning darky, as plainly as before. I thought then I would test the unreality of the apparition in another way. If it were an optical-illusion, the figure must recede as I advanced, or follow as I retreated. I accordingly advanced towards it; but, strange to say, it remained in the same spot, until I was within arm's length, when stretching forth my hand I grasped—nothing. I walked over the exact spot where the figure stood, and returned to my old stand, to be still more puzzled to see the figure in the same spot, with the same expression on its countenance, but with *both* arms hanging down by its side this time. More puzzled still, I retreated to see if it would follow; but no—there it stood still gazing after me. I took three or four turns up and down my beat, and on each return to the fallen tree beheld the figure in the same position as last seen. I then halted, determined to watch if other changes would manifest themselves in shadowy being before me. My comrade came towards me again, and I reiterated my former tale of the apparition. Still he couldn't see it. But, as I was yet talking of it, and still persisting I saw it, the phantom darky disappeared—not suddenly, but seeming to melt away gradually.

"He vanished in the darkness, like a beam
Of cold, gray moonlight in a wintry stream."

This is the first and only ghost I have ever had the pleasure of seeing, or, more properly speaking, fancying I saw. What caused its appearance I neither know nor care, and only relate the fact (or fancy) because I think it singular.

On a Sunday morning, about 10 o'clock, we started for Evans' Mills, to relieve Co. E, which had overstayed their time one week—doubtless from the fact that a large orchard of apple trees was upon the plantation, the fruit of which was a luxury they were loth to leave—small blame to them.

After a march of about two hours, we came out upon a clearing just beyond a continuation of the rebel line of defences to the right of the Beaufort railroad. Here we saw deserted houses, and a cotton gin; but no living creature of the human or brute creation, and the place looked solitary and deserted enough— its own sad elegy of war written plainly in the solitude which brooded over the absence of those who once gave animation to the scene, and made 'the wilderness blossom like the rose' with fields of cotton and gardens of bright flowers.

About a mile further on, after passing through a narrow belt of woods, we came out upon Evans' plantation. On our right was a field of some eighty acres, about half of which was covered with a young growth of apple trees. On the left was a field of about twenty acres, at the further end of which was the plantation house, with its negro huts, surrounded with the inevitable grove of elegant shade trees. Just opposite the front gate of the mansion, the road turned sharp to the right, and on looking ahead, we beheld a block-house, nearly completed, in the rear of which was the encampment, and our future abode. Upon reaching the block-house, the road took a turn to the left, down a short, steep hill, skirting the bank of a stream, which it crossed on a rude plank bridge, still turning toward the left. After crossing the bridge, a grist mill lay on the right, and about 60 yards on the left, on the dam of a magnificent pond of water stood a large saw mill, which ran two sets of saws when in operation. It was then idle, the dam having broke away. The road, after crossing the flume of the grist mill led on to the negro village—quite a collection of comfortable houses—built on each side of the cross road, which led to Pollocksville. Just before coming on to the Pollocksville road, in a field to the right was a large cotton gin and press. At the intersection of these roads was our outpost in the day time, the guard being drawn in to the mills at night.

The army wagons which accompanied, (with tents, cooking utensils, quartermasters' stores, company baggage, &c.,) arriving a few minutes after, the men soon had plenty to do in erecting tents, and fixing themselves as comfortably as circumstances would permit. There was a little board shanty with two bunks, lately occupied by the drummers of Co. E. To this my comrade and I 'froze'; and, having got our traps snugly bestowed—our guns and equipments slung up, and our blankets spread—we sallied forth in quest of plunder.

Our first raid was upon the orchard near by; but it had been picked bare. We, however, subjected every tree to a searching examination, and as the reward of our toil returned with about half a bushel of a apples. On our way back we passed through a small field of sweet potatoes, to which we returned with a sack, and soon were in possession of a bushel of very fine ones.

During our absence, foraging, the tents had all been put up, and the men were busy arranging their traps. Charley (our French cook) had not been idle meantime, and had a blazing fire, and coffee ready. Procuring from him a pot, we soon had the satisfaction of seeing some of the sweet potatoes, the fruits of our late raid, smiling upon us, and welcoming us to the feast. Giving the cook a couple of good ones for his accommodation, we retired to our cabin with our coffee, sweet potatoes and 'salt horse,' and made one of the most hearty and satisfactory meals I have ever known. Appetite was our best sauce, exercise had sharpened it, and the new and palatable food agreed so well with the disposition of the stomach, that it had ample satisfaction in embracing its best friend.

After eating, with pipe lit, I started forth to take a view of the mansion house, and its surroundings. On entering the front gate, I was struck with the size and beauty of an immense beech tree, whose wide extending branches covered a circle of over 100 feet in diameter—and, Yankee fashion, I immediately computed that if cut down it would make over five cords of firewood. It must have proved a cool and inviting shade for the planter and his family in the summer time. Approaching its huge trunk, I observed that the Yankee jacknife had been at work and covered it with the representative names of men from nearly every United States regiment that had ever been in the department. Besides the huge beech there were numerous other trees—elm, cedar, chaney—and the beautiful flowering althea.

The house was an ordinary two story one, containing about 7 rooms, set on brick blocks about three feet from the ground, and serving as a cool place of resort for the pigs, fowl, and youthful, curly-headed negroes, during the heat of the day. This, together with the plantation attached of some 10,000 acres, seven or eight hundred of which were cleared, together with the mills, and about 120 'head of darkies' (all of which excepting two old negroes and their wives, had been 'run up country'), belonged to a Mr. Evans, a son-in-law of Ex-Gov. Morehead, (after whom Morehead city had been named).

Evans was, as I afterwards found, a very influential man in that part of the country, and had early become a convert to the doctrine of secession. He raised a company of cavalry, and equipped them at his own expense. He took part in the battle of Newbern, and it must have been a bitter trial for him to leave so fine a property, though I believe he had another plantation in the upper part of the State. The regiment to which his company was attached, remained for some time in the State, and had more than one encounter with our cavalry. They were, however, finally ordered to join the army of Virginia, and were, no doubt, engaged in all its conflicts with our army. At the battle of Gettysburg, Evans, who had become a colonel, was wounded, taken prisoner, and died shortly after in hospital at Baltimore.

Such has been the fate of an infatuated man, who, like thousands of others, left a prosperous and comfortable home to plunge in the suicidal fray against the Government under which he was reared and had prospered. He may have repented his folly when too late; but I doubt it. Such men are as little given to repentance as they are to truth, justice and reason.

At the back of the mansion house were two negro huts, where those who were domestics lodged. The body of the negroes were lodged in the village before mentioned about a mile away. Doubtless there was design in this—as the master of bondmen must have lived as insecure amongst his slaves as the tyrant in the midst of his vassals.

Adjoining the negro-huts attached to the mansion were the various outhouses and stables, behind which the land sloped to waters of the tortuous stream which emptied into the mill-pond further down.

To my view Evans' Mills at first appeared a lonely place; but a further acquaintance with it materially altered my opinion. Were it not that the restraints which discipline imposes upon the soldier, living in this place would be quite agreeable. There was no lack of game of all kinds, from the red deer, the nocturnally rambling coon and possum, to the partridge, wild pigeons, grouse, waterfowl, and fish. The latter were the only legitimate sport for the soldiers (and many a finny inhabitant of those sluggish streams—though shy at times—graced his tin platter), as the necessities of war forbid the use of fire-arms upon any other game than men (butternuts—and some of them mighty hard nuts at that). Occasionally, however, the negroes, and such of the white inhabitants as were left behind 'when the rush of war was past,' with their coon dogs, and well provided with pine knots to guide them, would sally forth of a night and traverse the banks of the numerous streams and branches, and rarely would they proceed far until the peculiar bay of the dogs denoted that they had lit upon the track of a wary possum or coon, in the direction of which the hunters would hasten, to find the 'critter treed,' and if the tree was too large to cut down, one climbed, and with a club killed or dislodged him. A coon hunt has rarely been unsuccessful, from the great number of the 'animals' abounding, and the excellent training of the dogs, which seem to take after this kind of game as naturally as a cat takes after mice.

The streams are generally belted with fine groves of cedar, gum, black walnut, locust, and ash trees, intermixed, the whole bearing their proportion of parasites, some of which entwine themselves so closely round the trees they select to climb on as almost to become incorporated with them in the process of time, and look like huge serpents endeavoring to crush out their life but they look beautiful in the summer time, covered with leaves and fruit (for they are not all poisonous or profitless), and many a bunch of rich, purple grapes has the writer purloined from the midst of those masses of tangled creepers. This intermingling of hardwood trees with the evergreen pines had a pleasing effect upon me, as it recalled the remembrance of the northern forests where the pine, hemlock and spruce were often in the minority.

Occasionally, however, the explorer of these Southern woods, would suddenly come upon a cypress swamp, and he would there behold the incarnation of all that is dismal in a landscape, —especially if, as when I first beheld one, the time was just before twilight, and the slanting rays of the sun had ceased to penetrate the masses of the forest foliage. A picture, however finely wrought, would fail to give an idea of the utter gloom and funereal solemnity of such a scene; and if any lover or hater of humanity should wish to seek a solitude where, unmolested, he could mourn over the wickedness and folly of mankind, and make himself thoroughly miserable, I would advise him to select a spot in full view of a cypress swamp,—and if he will not suffer enough, do enough penance, and weep enough to wash out and atone for the world's sins—his own included,—in the space of the twelve months, then it will not be the fault of the swamp, I can vouch. I do not wonder that the ancients, even aside from their superstitions, selected the cypress as an emblem of death and mourning—for no one can behold that tree in its native solitude and state without thinking of all the friends he had lost, and would be likely to lose for the next hundred years.—Picture to yourself, gentle reader, the bed of a sluggish stream, enriched by the accumulations of vegetable mould for unknown ages, until the water forced itself through a deep, narrow channel, winding hither and thither; that at a former indefinite period, the seeds deposited on this mould germinated, and there arose from its slimy depths, like ghosts that had 'burst their cerements,' the mighty cypress trees; that they continued to grow slowly upward, but toward the base the trunks swelled to undue proportions like the paunches of gluttons—and undoubtedly the cypress is the glutton among trees, as its huge cone-shaped roots are well adapted to the ravenous absorption of air, and the rich liquified food that is forever in process of formation around and above them. And thus they tower up in the midst of their slimy abode, huge, bilious and bloated, and look like a grim array of fallen spirits, which, having attempted to cross into daylight, got stuck in the mud of their mythical Styx.

Such is a cypress swamp.

In nationality the men of Co. K comprised Americans, Canadians, Provincials, English, Irish, Scotch, French and Germans. In disposition and character, they were nearly as diverse as their nationality; but taken as specimens of the countries they represented, were about as intelligent and respectable a body of men as could well be expected from such material.

The Captain, Joseph R. Simonds, (for many years a bookbinder in Spring Lane, Boston,) was a thoroughly patriotic and honest man, a good soldier, with many virtues, and a few faults and foibles (and what man has not these to a greater or less extent.) He took great pride in the well-being and efficiency of his company; and its good name, and the praise of his superiors for cleanliness, superiority in drill, or having a small sick-list, were to him matters of just pride and gratulation,—and frequently, after a creditable performance on drill or parade, he would snap his fingers with delight, and, after dismissal, invite them all to his quarters for a treat. He was careful about the quality of their food, and whenever he could (which was not often) would procure such articles of luxury and dietic change as would be most likely to promote health. He was uniformly kind, obliging and considerate, and did not look upon his men as mere pieces of mechanism that moved when he pulled the wires. He considered them *men*,—socially his equals, though in reality under his command, and, to a certain extent at his mercy. He rarely abused his authority—never maliciously; and though he occasionally did injustice to some deserving men—it was, I think, more from an error of judgment than through design. Yet he was popular and unpopular with the men. Soldiers like sailors will grumble, and it is a privilege they often abuse; but, the fit over, they all invariably acknowledged his worth, and disposition to treat them well.

The first Lieut. (J. A. Greeley) was of a quiet disposition, a strict (but not over strict) disciplinarian, and a man of considerable genius in engineering (he subsequently had the planning and superintendence of several fortifications near Newbern). He was a strict temperance man, and wished the men to practice this virtue also. He has since been detached from the regiment, and commissioned captain in the 2d regiment of Heavy Artillery.

But I cannot enumerate the names of all the company,—and will content myself with mentioning a few of the 'characters'—and the first that occurs to my mind is "old Jesse Hitchings" (forgive me, Jesse, for putting your name in print; but you need be no more ashamed of it than you were of your old cap riddled by the enemy's bullets). Jesse was a character—a tall, thin old bachelor of over fifty—of a pleasant, benevolent disposition, a good soldier, an uncompromising patriot (no *compromises* with the rebels, was his motto)—and a successful hand at poker. It is related of Jesse, that when the company was doing picket duty at the Deep Gully, he lit a fire one night at the outpost, and when his time came to mount guard, leisurely walked up and down in front of the fire, giving the enemy's pickets a fair chance, if so disposed, to pick him off—and upon being warned of his danger, cooly replied—

"Well, if I'm to be shot I'll be shot, I suppose—what's the odds."

In camp, on guard, in the bivouac of the battle-field, wherever there was a fire, Jesse could be seen at any hour of the night bending over the same, his chin resting between his knees, warming his long skinny hands—sometimes asleep; but mostly half awake or dozing. Poor Jesse—he is one of the few sterling men who act well their part without ostentation, and are rarely noticed for their real worth.

Another character was "Billy Patterson" (he was called "Billy," though his name was James). He was a hard-working, rough-spoken fellow (his general salutation being "G' along till haal wi' ye!") Billy, though a good soldier, and brave in action, did not like guard or picket duty—and, being an excellent cook, generally contrived by a species of finesse—not always of an unexceptionable character—to work himself into a good berth, with pots for his jolly companions. Charley (our French cook) shortly after going to Evans' Mills fell sick, and Billy took his place—which he held afterwards for a long time, and flourished and bullied when sober, and when drunk abused every one—and gave the mess very good dinners.

Sam Kenny was another whom I considered a character. He was nicknamed 'Dickens,' being a great admirer of that author. 'Dickens' was an intelligent man, but fond of whiskey; and whenever he imbibed too much was sure to get into some scrape or other, which generally ended in depositing him in the guard-house. It is related of him, that being one night in Newbern, on a 'bender,' he applied for admission into a house (where he was acquainted), but the lady noticing his condition, refused; when, after repeated failures to get in, becoming convinced of the uselessness of any further trial, and by way of revenge, he put his mouth to the keyhole, and shouted—

"I say, madam, do you chew snuff?"

Now be it known that snuff chewing is quite a common practice among the women in and around Newbern, and for aught I know is a regular Southern institution; but those of any pretension to refinement never use it, or if they do, it is on the sly—and a greater insult could not be offered a woman than to ask her if she chewed snuff. 'Dickens,' no doubt, had his revenge.

A young fellow, named J. E. Mills, had a mania for cutting his autograph upon trees, walls, fences, and objects in every place he visited. It is related that during a freshet, when a lot of logs in the river above the dam broke loose, every one of them contained one or more inscriptions of "J. E. M.," cut in with an axe or knife.

William Stack ' was a soldier every inch of him.' He had been in the British service over ten years, and served in India. His peculiarities were numerous; but were redeemed by a strict integrity, a love of duty and a thorough knowledge of his business. I often wondered why men, his inferiors in many of the most essential qualifications of a soldier, were promoted over him, while he remained a private. He entertained a great veneration for the British army—and thought the British soldier not only superior, but better paid, better clothed, and better cared for than the American soldier. He had a good memory, a rich fund of anecdote, and many a weary hour has he beguiled by the relation of scenes and adventures in 'the land of the palm and the poppy.'

John Smith was another who had served in the British army. He was a good soldier, an unpretending man, and the pertinacity with which he defended the government, (there are two parties in the army as well as here), his strong anti-slavery sentiments when nearly all were down on the poor negro, and the confidence he felt in the ultimate success of our cause, even in the darkest hours when the general opinion prevailed that we could never whip the South, might well put to shame many of his American comrades, who often seemed to lose in their desire for peace, the consciousness that it was their's to dictate the terms to a beaten foe. The poor fellow has been taken prisoner —and is now in Dixie.

Smith had a brother who was nicknamed 'Ben-Doza.' 'Ben' was discharged in March, 1863, and I gave him a curious stick which I cut in one of the swamps to bring home for me. If this should meet his eye, I wish he would hasten to ' fork it over.'

But lest I should become tedious and uninteresting, I will drop the biographical and take up the chronological thread of my yarn, noticing the different individuals as they may be brought by circumstances into future scenes. It is true that in speaking of the mere rank and file of the army, I do not write of men known to fame. There is, indeed, little of romance connected with the private soldier—that peculiar species of flummery (which makes the heart of the dreamy damsel of sixteen flutter so) being, as it were by right divine, the speciality of the ideal mustached, lightning-eyed, and so forth young men of the shoulder straps. Those I write of principally occupy, many of them, the humblest (though the most useful) position in our grand army. It is such men who do the real fighting, and have to take and give the hardest knocks—and if a score of those brave hearts are laid low by the hand of war, it creates not half as much public sensation as the destruction of an old barn by fire, or the escape of a negro from rebeldom. Their biography is written by the orderly sergeant in a few words, and their requiem sung by the turkey-buzzard out on a foraging expedition. Their names, it is true, are on the rolls of fame; but who cares for these, except it be their immediate friends and relatives—and the clerks in the pension-bureau, who mayhap think it particularly unkind in privates A. B. or C. to die at all, and thus give them so much additional labor.

Two brothers, named Tibbetts, living about three miles beyond our outpost, lost some hogs and cattle in a very mysterious way, and came into our lines to inquire if we knew anything of them. Of course we didn't, and Billy Patterson's pots never told tales. I entered into conversation with one of the brothers, who appeared to be a civil sort of a man, and who invited me among others to visit his house, saying that he had plenty of eggs, &c., and could get up a very good dinner for us.

I remembered Tibbetts' invitation, and a few days after, accompanied by a companion, started out to see him. He lived in a miserable log cabin, about 20 feet square, without windows, having shutters to supply their place at night, which were opened in the day time to admit light and air. A field of about

25 acres surrounded the domicile, partly planted in corn and peas, with about three acres of sweet potatoes. And these, with a few pigs, and a small garden, constituted this family's whole 'visible means of support.' The family consisted of a sallow, bilious-looking wife (all women thereabouts, as well as men, look alike) and a half-dozen sallow, bilious-looking children. (Nearly all the natives of that level, swampy region are thin, and have a shaky appearance.)

I noticed, to my surprise, upon my first introduction to Madam Tibbetts, that a small stick protruded about two inches from her mouth, and that ever and anon she spat out what seemed marvellously like tobacco juice. I watched her movements for some time during our conversation, and I noticed that she occasionally removed the stick from her mouth, and, one end being made soft by chewing, dipped the same into a box of snuff, replaced it again, and ran it around her gums and teeth in the same manner as one would use a tooth-brush. I found that neither Tibbetts or his wife, nor his brother or sister (the latter a smiling old maid) who afterwards joined us, could read or write—in fact it was considered quite out of their line altogether, though they seemed to regret that their children could not have some education. They were a fair specimen of that class of settlers at the South known as 'poor whites.'

Being allowed, when off duty, a free range within the lines, our visits were made in all directions—sometimes (often, I confess) transgressing our orders, we went beyond, especially towards the abodes of the Messrs. Tibbetts—and we frequently stumbled upon a quiet household of 'poor whites,' who received us civilly, though by no means graciously. All of these were, however, strongly 'secesh' in feeling, having had their minds pretty thoroughly poisoned with the false tales told them by their late 'superiors' of Yankee injustice and cupidity.

In conversation with the elder Tibbetts, I learned that the

honey-bees often selected the trunks of hollow trees in which to gather immense deposits of honey, and that in going up a creek lately he had discovered a tree, which he intended visiting some time. The idea of a 'bee hunt' was novel to me, and I determined to join him; and, a few days after, with a comrade, started for Tibbetts' house, who readily undertook to pilot us upon our saccharine expedition.

We were successful in getting a considerable amount of honey; but staid out so late that the officers became alarmed at our absence, thinking we were 'gobbled up' by the 'rebs,' and doubled the guard, served out extra ammunition, &c.,—and when we did come in at last, reprimanded us for staying out so long, and forbid any of the men going beyond the lines in future.

Time wore on. At first we expected a recall at the end of each week after our time had expired, but no such order came, and as the season was beginning to wear the sear and yellow leaf in its garments, and the indications of cold weather warned, us that the time was at hand when

"The wild deer and wolf to their covert" must "flee,"

we bethought us that the negro village might abound in material of which shanties might be erected, and, as Billy Patterson. elegantly expressed it, "be a d—d sight more comfortable than miserable." This bright thought was slow in spreading, and it was not until three or four men of a mess erected a snug shanty, that it took root and flourished—and then there was a rush for the 'diggins.'

The shanties at the outpost, once the shelter of the humble household gods of many a smoky descendant of Ham, were threatened with disembowelment—until the fury of the onslaught was turned upon the cotton gin, which soon presented a skeleton appearance. The plundered boards and scantling had to be carried by the men half a mile. But they set to work

with a will. For at least two weeks nothing could be heard
around the camp, from sunrise to the going down thereof, but
hammer and saw, and saw and hammer, and from the promiscuous heaps of purloined boards and scantling there arose in
due time one of the most curious villages that could be met with
outside of negrodom; but they were as comfortable as could be
desired, and well laid out with bunks, gunracks, &c. Each had
a flue or chimney for a stove or fireplace, the bricks to build
which had to be carried on the back, or wheeled by hand from
a mile and a half to two miles; and as wood was plenty, we
never lacked for good fires. Thus comfortably situated, it was
no wonder that we became attached to Evans' Mills.

It being designed to erect permanent barracks in the vicinity
of Newbern, and the steam saw mill in that city proving insuffi-
cient to supply enough lumber—workmen being plenty, a
detail from any of the New England regiments supplying any
number needed—it was resolved to repair the broken dam at
Evans' Mills. A detachment of about sixty contrabands, under
the superintendence of a sort of Baron Munchausen chap, a
private in a New York artillery regiment—was sent to make the
necessary repairs.

The dam had broke away at the waste water gate—and the
genius who was sent to repair it, commenced by filling in the
waste gate with brushwood and earth—and, after a month's
labor, (costing the Government over $1,500), he succeeded in
partially stopping the water, so that a few thousand feet of
boards could be sawed; but the first rain-storm swelled the dam
so much that, having no proper outlet for the superabundant
water to escape, it gave way, and the blundering fool and his
work departed about the same time—the former to hospital
sick, and the latter to be distributed along the oozy bottom of the
tortuous creek which emptied into the Trent River.

When the rebels were defeated at Newbern, Evans, like

other large planters, sent all his slaves to a plantation which he owned in the upper part of the State—that is, all who were worth sending, for he left two old negroes and their wives behind to 'take charge' of the plantation. These, in process of time, and the occupation of the place by our forces, were joined by others, until the negro population at the time our company went there, amounted to about ten, including picaninnies. The old negroes alluded to were called respectively, Old (Uncle) George, and Indian Joe. The former venerable old patriarch was "eighty-five, sar," communicative and religious, and the latter a cross between the Negro and Indian—retaining a good deal of the aboriginal physique and character—respectful, but retiring in his manner; and, though said to be fully as old as George, was spry and supple, a good hand at a tar-kiln, and a keen sportsman, never going to the woods without being accompanied by his dogs and an old Harper's Ferry musket—

"For you know de coons come out sometimes 'fore dark, and de deer dey stray off up dar down here in de day, and dey's good eatin', I reckon, is dem deers."

"I suppose you would not hesitate to pink a rebel if he should come across you instead of a deer, Joe?"

"Lor, yes—no—reckon—(scratching his head). O yes—right good day, sar—good morning, sar."

I think he'd shoot—if the alternative was to shoot or be taken.

The other contrabands were mostly runaways. One of them, a mulatto, was a good carpenter, a man of some intelligence, and interested me much. His story was simple, and illustrated the atrocious system, which subverts honor, and makes conscience a tool to be used as interest may dictate. He was 'raised' (that is the term, and sounds odd when applied to human beings) up country, and when his old master died he left him free; but the son and heir not liking to lose a 'right smart boy' of his description, would not give him his freedom, but kept him as a slave, treating him precisely like the other bondmen. When the war broke out, his master, who resided or did business at Wilmington, joined the navy, as captain of a gunboat, and took this slave with him as his servant. After the battle of Roanoke, when our gunboats followed up and destroyed the rebel fleet, his master, when one of our gunboats ran into the one he commanded, deserted him, jumping overboard, to escape capture; but, while in the water, a stray shot struck him, and he 'sank to rise no more.' The mulatto, glad of the change that gave him his liberty, accompanied our forces to Newbern, and there remained, entered the employ of the Government, and performed his part in a skillful and faithful manner.

Another of the contrabands was a full-blooded African negro, bearing the classical name of Nero. He was from Duplin County, some ninety miles north of Newbern, and near the Virginia line, and had run away from a cruel master, as numerous scars on his person testified, travelling the entire distance on foot through woods and swamps, and subsisting upon an occasional ear of corn, for which he ventured into the fields only at night, eluding the rebel patrols and pickets, and, finally, almost exhausted and worn out, he arrived, with about five or six others from the same place, inside our picket lines, and gave himself up. He left behind him a wife and six children; but notwithstanding this, and the stories he had heard of Yankee barbarity to runaway negroes (the slaves being generally told that the Yankees placed iron rigs through the shoulder-blades of the darkies, and sold them off to Cuba), he was willing to run all risks for the bare chance of obtaining his liberty; and, he said, if the other slaves knew how well the contrabands were treated, they would come in in greater numbers. His simple story would fill an interesting volume. When Wild's brigade was subsequently organized, he joined the first regiment, and, I have no doubt, has proved himself a capital soldier. Wo to the rebels that fell in his power. He had many wrongs to avenge, and would avenge them, if opportunity offered.

Uncle George was a good specimen of the ideal negro—fat, good-natured, and seemingly contented.

"Well, uncle," I said, "how do you like the Yankees?"

"Right well, sar—dey's bery fine people, sar!"

"Would you sooner be with the Yankees than the rebs?"

"O yes, sar; (my name's George, sar); 'cause I'se a free man now, and dat's what I am now, sar."

"You think you are free now, and that the Yankees made you free, do you?"

"O yes, sar," he replied, and then added, in a deeply impressive voice—"and I tank de Lord and you Yankees for dat. De ole man hab worked for many years—de good Lord he send me and the ole woman six sons and five daughters, and massa, he sell some off afore de war, take some away when de Yankees come—and now, de poor ole man and de poor ole woman am left all alone in de world; but de good Lord send de Yankees, and dey make us free afore we die, and dat am payment enough for all ole George's work—bress de Lord, amen"

George finding, I suppose, that I took an interest in him, and did not treat him as it might be inferred many would from their salutation of "Hello, old nig—how dye *do*," often visited our shanty at dinner-time, and we had always plenty of crackers and 'salt horse,' and an occasional pint of soup or coffee to spare him; but the cook (Billy Patterson,) perhaps from pure good nature, took a fancy to old George, and he soon forsook our more humble board for the savory flesh-pots of Billy's cookhouse, perfectly satisfied to be addressed as you 'd——d old nigger,' so long as he had his revenge in the shape of a plentiful supply of good grub.

I stated before that the outpost guard was drawn in at night to the mills (the day-guard at the mills being camp-guard at night). A few darkies, who worked for the government making tar and cutting saw logs, lodged in the mill. Without education enough to read, without the knowledge of the commonest accessories of amusement, it cannot be wondered that the time hung heavily upon their hands; but their naturally elastic temperaments stood them in good need, and suggested a species of amusement to pass away the time that was best suited to their capacity, viz.: dancing and its promoter, 'jigging'—a species of vocal and pantomimic music almost peculiar to the African race. At first their levees were attended only by gents of color; but, by and by, the spirit of their performances began to spread, and soldiers from the relief guard and the camp visited them, and enjoyed hugely the sight of the dancing, sweating darkies, (encouraging and applauding the most expert—and there were many supple legs and nimble feet among them), and the equally sweating and nimble 'jiggers' or time-beaters. The 'jiggers' did not always depend upon the voice, but used it as a sort of auxiliary or flourish to their time-beating, which latter was performed by striking the open hands upon the thighs, legs and breast, and together in rapid succession, and in admirable measure, so that the tune thus beat could be followed by the dancer as precisely as if played upon a full band.

We had a Maryland negro in our company, who ran away from his master, and became attached to the regiment in Baltimore. He was called 'Pomp'—a lithe, supple fellow—and, with a few months training, I have no doubt, would equal, if not surpass, some of the clog-dancers of our friends the Morris Bro's. It was amusing to note the patronizing airs he adopted towards the North Carolina 'nigs,' and, I presume, the circumstances of his having come from Maryland, and being so long in the army, added not a little to obtain for him a certain kind of prestige among his simple sable brethren. The soldiers for amusement taught him the manual of arms, and so naturally did he take to the business that it was a common remark among the men that there were few better drilled men in the command than Pomp. But Pomp became lazy and independent, and left the company shortly after we went to Evans' Mills to work for Government. But his mind was not in work, and after a few weeks labor he went to Newbern, and there became attached to a company of the 43d Mass. regiment, as Captain's servant. This captain (I know not his name, or I should record it, to his credit), taught him as well as some other negroes, to read and write; and, when the policy of the Government, directing the enlistment of the blacks, reached North Carolina, Wild's brigade began to be formed, Pomp was among the first to enlist, and, for his proficiency in drill, and quickness for military duty, he was made a sergeant in the North Carolina colored regiment.

"I've been made free by de President of my country," he said to me, when I met and congratulated him upon joining the army, "and I tink it is my duty to fight for de country dat makes me a free man."

This regiment afterwards bore a prominent part in the unfortunate battle of Olustee, Florida. I wonder if poor Joe (he changed Pomp to Joseph) escaped.

On the 28th of August, the 17th reg't embarked on transports for the purpose of capturing Plymouth; but upon arriving opposite that town, found the place too well defended to warrant a landing, and they returned without disembarking.

On the 30th of October, the 17th regiment left Newbern on board steamers, and proceeded up the Neuse River about eight miles, where they were joined by cavalry, artillery, and a large baggage train, the whole under command of Colonel Amory. They landed and marched to Swift Creek, a small settlement eight miles distant, which was reached at sundown. Here they were fired upon by the rebel cavalry picket, who had destroyed the bridge over the creek. They fled upon our approach. The following forenoon was employed by our forces in building the bridge, and at noon the column was again in motion towards Washington, N. C., which our forces reached on the evening of November 1st, without molestation.

November 2d, the line of march was again continued, (our forces being augmented by the addition of several thousand infantry,) in the direction of Williamston. Towards sundown the advance came up with the enemy, posted behind entrenchments, at a place called Rawle's Mills, who disputed their passage; but our forces soon compelled them to retreat, and the following morning the advance again continued on to Williamston, which place the column reached at noon, having marched a distance of twenty-three miles from Washington. Leaving the sick and foot-sore on board the gunboats in the river, the troops marched out of the town about three miles, and bivouacked for the night.

November 4th, they took up the line of march for Hamilton, within two miles of which they were obliged to halt for several hours to build a bridge, near which was a deserted breastwork, leading from the woods across the main road to a fort on the river bank. Hamilton was reached about sundown, and, like Williamston, was found entirely deserted. The town being set on fire by the troops, the sick were placed on board gunboats, and the expedition marched out of Hamilton several miles, and bivouacked for the night.

November 5th, they started early in the morning, taking the road to Tarboro'—marched until night, when they came to a halt, and bivouacked within nine miles of Tarboro'. The following morning they commenced their return march, not having met with the enemy in any force. A heavy rain having set in, the roads were in a bad condition, and the marching much harder than it had been previously. The expedition reached Hamilton late in the afternoon, and took up their quarters for the night in the deserted dwellings.

November 7th, a violent snow storm raged in the morning, but it did not delay the march, which was continued for Williamston, by a road leading near the river, and which they had not travelled before. No force of the enemy appeared to interrupt the march, and the expedition reached Williamston in the afternoon, where it remained until the morning of the 9th, when the line of march was taken up for Plymouth, N. C., a distance of twenty-three miles. They reached the latter place the next morning, 10th, and Newbern on the 11th, at noon, having been absent thirteen days, and having marched about 150 miles. The expedition captured about 50 prisoners, 400 horses and mules, and about 100 teams.

The failure of this expedition, and the causes of its failure, are pretty well known, and need no comment from me, save that it caused much hardship to the troops comprising it, and left Newbern in an almost defenceless state. The rebels, judging that the garrison of the city had been largely drawn upon (but never dreaming that this was the case to so great an extent), to divert, perhaps, whatever after purposes our commanders had, and to make them recall the troops as fast as possible, sent a weak force to demonstrate in front of Newbern. This drove in our pickets, and created the utmost apprehension in the city. The case seemed critical, and every available man was called inside the defences to await the onslaught of the enemy.

Our company (the remainder of the regiment being in the expedition,) received hurried orders to report in Newbern, and rumors coming in heralded the enemy as advancing upon the city in large numbers. The order to pack up and be ready to march at a minute's warning, was received by us just as we were 'turning in,' and was not very welcome news you may be sure, but to hear was to obey; and in half an hour we were ready for the road, and some talked of the morrow, what the 'row' was all about, whether we should have a fight, and others (myself among the number) went to bed and slept. About three o'clock in the morning I was aroused from a pleasant sleep by my comrades, and heard all around me the hurried tramp of men. Hastily putting on my knapsack, I seized my gun, and went forth to take my place in the line. The night was foggy, and a feeble moon, while it brightened the obscurity a little, lent to the half distinct scene a dreary and confused appearance. A few men had been detailed to destroy the bridge; and the strokes of the axe, the falling of the planks and beams into the water, the hum of the camp—its lights glancing to and fro, contrasted with the solemnity of the surrounding silence (which only echoed noises of our hasty departure, or the hoot of the owl) left a cheerless impression on my mind.

After a march of two hours, we reached our old camp tired and exhausted, to be refreshed by a good dipper of coffee.

The morning advanced but the rebels came not; and as reinforcements arrived by the railroad from Beaufort, all apprehensions of the result of an attack upon the city died out, and the day wore away without any demonstration being made against any part of our lines. Indeed, word came in from our scouts, that the rebels had fallen back, satisfied, no doubt, with having carried out their design of creating a diversion, which would serve to hasten the recall of the expedition.

In the evening we received orders to return to Evans' Mills, which place we reached by nightfall.

What must have been the surprise and dismay of the darkies to work on the mill-dam (who knew nothing of our departure during the night, although we made noise enough to rouse the 'seven sleepers') upon waking in the morning to find the bridge destroyed and the camp deserted. We were told that they no sooner heard of our departure—and the reports, greatly exaggerated, no doubt, of a rebel attack upon Newbern—than, considering it was 'all up' with them, they scattered, and made for the woods—'every man for himself, and the devil take the hindmost.' Some of them turned up in the vicinity of Newbern, others made their way to Morehead City and Beaufort, while others were never heard from, and these, it was thought likely, being too frightened to venture out in the clearings, supposing the whole country again in possession of the rebels, were starved to death, or lost their way, and came out somewhere in Dixie—no doubt into the lion's mouth they were trying to avoid.

Poor unfortunates, the sport of every varying breeze of fortune, good or ill. The best fortune for them is as yet but indifferent, while ill fortune is death. They are, alas, no 'chosen people of God.' They have no Moses to organize and lead them out of their land of bondage; no cloud by day or pillar of fire by night to guide them; no ark of their freedom's covenant around which to rally [yes, the starry flag is their ark, and, thank Heaven, wherever it waves over them they are free!] No miracles are vouchsafed for their preservation; no manna from heaven; no quails; no water gushing from the rock to assauge their thirst. Alas! alas! that their pathway to freedom should be beset with so many dangers—that its course should so often lead them through the valley of the shadow of death! Poor creatures! heaven help them through the fiery ordeal in which they are passing!

The old darkies, however, belonging to the mill, together with the others who had not been there when we came, did not skedaddle; but, by turns, kept a good look-out on the Pollocksville road, ready, of course, to leave at the approach of the rebels, though determined not to do so until they hove in sight. Old George took charge of our camp, closed every door, and when we returned, every article we were forced to leave behind, even to the smallest and most trivial, remained just as we had left it.

Back once more in our comfortable quarters, and resuming our old routine of duty, we began to think that we were as good as settled for the winter. Our old pastimes were revived—rambling, fishing, quoit pitching playing cards, backgammon, and draughts. The same huge fires were kindled and burned brightly in front of our quarters, and at the outposts, for the guards to warm themselves by in the dreary watches of the chilly night, around which, before retiring to rest, groups of smoking men assembled, and spun many a yarn of strange adventure in all lands, from the orient to the occident, and from the frozen regions of the north to the trackless southern seas—mostly true, I believe, but surely entertaining.

This state of affairs lasted a few weeks longer, when suddenly we received orders to rejoin the regiment, which took the place of the Mass. 23d in doing the provost duty at Newbern. This was about the 20th of November. To some this change was delightful, while to others (and I was one of these) it was not a welcome change. But we packed up—this time with more deliberation—and the next morning when Co. A, 23d regiment, Captain Brewster, came to relieve us were ready to evacuate, leaving everything connected with the camp to our successors, in apple-pie order. I wish they could (or did) return the compliment; but they did not, and were so 'put out' about being put out of Newbern, that they vented their spleen upon the luckless houses occupied by them as quarters, smashing up every thing that might conduce to the comfort of their successors.

Our quarters were on Pollock street, near the market and the office of the Provost Marshal. Co. B's quarters adjoined ours, and F occupied quarters on the other side of the street nearly opposite. After considerable labor in sweeping, scrubbing, making bunks, &c., we became settled down once more,

## DELIGHTS OF PROVOST DUTY. 61

comfortable enough. But our duty was no child's play. We were on guard every second day—the intermediate one being filled up (twice a week) by a march of six miles and a brigade drill of three hours or more. This did not leave much time to ourselves, after cleaning boots, polishing brasses and buttons, and brushing clothes, for we had to appear neat and tidy while on duty.

A provost guard is a kind of police-soldier, and his duties are as multifarious as the character of his office and power is indefinite. His instructions vary in detail from day to day; and, before he goes on duty for the day has a string of orders and regulations, as long as the laws of the Medes and Persians, read to him, often couched in language that could be defined to mean one thing or another, or nothing at all in particular. For example, the guard is told to examine *all* passes and salute *all* officers; to permit no fast driving; to allow no soldier or man-o'-war sailor to go by him unless provided with passes properly countersigned; to allow no citizen to pass after a certain hour, without a special permit from the provost marshal; to 'jug' every negro found out after 9 P.M.; to allow no citizen or negro to be abused; to allow no breach of the peace; to permit no horses to be tied to trees; to stop all disturbances whatever indoors or out of doors; to, in fact, keep his eyes 'peeled,' and be continually on the alert, and, if possible, do all the impossible things required of him. Four hours on post (and twice posted) performing this delightful duty, was required of the man detailed for guard. The accommodations at the guard-houses were abominable. The windows were broken, the bunks smashed up, poor fires, and the floors so dirty, and the cricks and crevices around so filled with vermin that one night's experience in the endeavor to get rest in them was generally sufficient to deter most of those who still retained the idea that cleanliness was a virtue from ever attempting the like again.

Major Frankle of the 17th regiment was Provost Marshal, and was a worthy successor of Col. Kurtz, of the 23d (now Chief of Police in Boston.)

I cannot enter into a relation of all the incidents which enlivened the monotony of our provost duty in Newbern, not from lack of good material—that would, perhaps, make thirty or forty pages of readable matter, but want of space admonishes me that it will not pay. Suffice it to say that, with forty or fifty thousand men in the department, a large proportion of whom were in the vicinity of Newbern—the 17th had their hands full, and the lock-up often became overcrowded, as did the jails in time. We had drunken men to arrest—street rows to quell, horse-racings, shootings and stabbings to look after—brawls in bad houses to put a stop to, and arrest drunken and half-crazed men armed to the teeth, and other duty of a no less dangerous character to perform. But I believe we did things 'up to the handle;' in fact I'm certain we did—notwithstanding there were many complaints (as there always must be in such cases) and criticisms of our method of procedure.

To add to our already heavy labor, shortly after we were in the city, the marine battalion (which I have before incidentally spoken of,) had refused to do further duty, and were placed in our custody. These gallant fellows had been shamefully used. When enlisted in New York city, they were promised $18 per month for the privates, or sailors, and pay in proportion for the petty officers. They had been in the service over a year, had not received any pay, clothing, or allowances for the same, and were informed that they would not be recognized in any other capacity than soldiers, with whom they must consider themselves on an equal footing in pay, as in all other respects. Considering this a violation of agreement, they refused as a body to shoulder a musket or do any kind of duty, and thus passively mutinied. The men of the 17th pitied the poor fellows, and showed them many acts of kindness. The Major, too, while he had to enforce their imprisonment, sympathized with the marines, and, I have reason to believe, did all in his power to have their just claims considered, and their wrongs righted; but the knot on the 'red tape' which bound the poor fellows could not be opened, and it was not cut. So, after a two month's imprisment, they were given the choice of servitude in the forts as criminals, or the alternative of enlisting in the navy, and they wisely accepted the alternative. I think their's was a case of peculiar hardship. Some of those human kites which abound in large cities started the project of their enlistment, without the approval of the Government, made money out of the affair, and left their victims to curse them for many a weary heartburn, many an anxious, hopeless thought of home, and of a perhaps destitute family.

One of Co. K's men, named Finn, at one time a guard over the marines, allowed two of them to go out to purchase something at the market, but the Major, somehow, discovered the charitable error, and rushing up to the guard, said:

"Vat for you let ze marines go away?"

"But they'll come back again, sir."

"O—fool—fool—I vill have you put under arrest and court-mars*hal!*"

Soon after the marines returned, and Finn, who caught sight of the Major passing, sung out—

"They're back again, Major! The marines"—

But the Major, who was in a hurry, passed him by, angrily exclaiming—

"O fool—fool—o-h block-head!"

"Be jabers," said Finn, looking after the Major, but taking care he was not heard by that officer,—"ye're the first man that ever called me so far out of my name that I didn't lay on the broad of his back!"

There were four other Massachusetts regiments in the department, viz :—the 23d, 24th, 25th, and 27th.

The 23d regiment, Col. Kurtz, was recruited in Lynnfield, which place it left for Annapolis, Md., on the 11th of November, 1861, and reached there on the 16th; and on January 6th, 1862, embarked upon transports as a portion of Gen. Burnside's Expedition to North Carolina.

The regiment, after encountering the fearful storms off Hatteras, was among the first to land on Roanoke Island, and in the engagements which followed bore a conspicuous and honorable part. It then accompanied the expedition up the Neuse, and took an active part in the battle of Newbern (March 14th, 1862), where it lost ten killed (including its Lieut. Colonel, Merritt) and forty-one wounded.

The 23d afterwards did picket duty, and took part in nearly all the expeditions into the interior and along the sea-coast.

On May 7th, the 23d relieved the 25th Mass. regiment doing provost duty in Newbern, where it continued until Nov. 20th, when it was in turn relieved by the 17th.

In January, the 23d formed part of the expedition to South Carolina, but did nothing, owing to a misunderstanding between Gens. Foster and Hunter, and returned, in April to North Carolina, and encamped at a place called Carolina City, near Morehead City.

Later it was transferred to Norfolk, and, I believe, is at present in that portion of the department.

The 23d bears the reputation of being a good regiment, and stands high on the roll of honor. Success to the old 23d.

The 24th Mass. regiment, Col. Stevenson, was recruited at Readville, and formed part of the Burnside expedition to North Carolina, and in the battles of Roanoke Island and Newbern, acted a conspicuous and noble part. This regiment, in common with others, had its share of marching on expeditions and doing picket duty (in which it had several sanguinary engagements with the enemy, who were invariably defeated). It accompanied Gen. Foster to South Carolina, where it has added fresh laurels to its name, as well as in Florida, where it remained until April last. The 24th is a splendid regiment. It is now in the army of the Potomac, and has shared in the triumphs which have at length rewarded that long-suffering but noble and brave army—that has at length came 'out of the wilderness.'

The 25th regiment, Col. Upton, was raised in the western part of the State, and left Camp Lincoln, Worcester, to join Burnside, and take part in his expedition. Little need be said, save that this regiment has inscribed on its banners such names as 'Roanoke Island,' 'Newbern,' 'Kinston,' 'Whitehall,' 'Goldsboro,' &c., &c. This regiment did the first provost duty in North Carolina. The 25th has taken part—together with the 23d and 27th—in the late brilliant advance of Gen. Butler on Richmond, where it has come in for its share of glory and hard knocks.

The 27th, Col. Lee, was also raised in the western part of the State, and left Springfield Jan. 6th, and joined Burnside's troops at Annapolis, Md. The 27th shared in all the battles, marches, and picket-skirmishes in North Carolina. In fact, the history of one of these regiments is the history of the whole. All, alike, have a glorious record, and have earned the same by the hardest kind of fighting, marching and suffering.

In October, the first of the nine months regiments began to arrive. The 44th was, I believe, the first of these—a fine-looking body of men; but seeming more like a regiment of officers than soldiers. Their style of dress, though about the same as the 'regulation,' varied in being of a much finer texture, and containing, at least, two more buttons on the tails of their dress coats than the regulation allowed to privates. (Orders were issued during our stay in the city to cut off the extra buttons, and much ill-feeling was created by the remorseless cur-*tail*-ment practiced by the men of the Seventeenth towards their fellow-soldiers of the 44th.) Some of the men, too, seemed to possess a consciousness of their superiority, induced, no doubt, by their fancied higher social standing at home, and passed the poor three-years men with the same patronizing and patrician air, their eye-glasses clasped upon their noses in the same manner, as when strutting amid their fathers' workmen in Massachusetts, or when promenading the thoroughfares, and ogling the girls (beg pardon, young ladies) at home. It is true they were civil, and mostly well-behaved young men; but their civility, though well intended, was bestowed with a hauteur which had an opposite effect, and left rankling in the minds of their less favored comrades (all soldiers are comrades) a feeling of envy and, perhaps, disgust. Undoubtedly, there were men in this regiment of a very high order of intellect; but there was a class among them composed of puny clerks and school-boys, whose notions of the world and what constituted a man were about as crude as those of any apron-string hero could be; and it was the influence of this class operating as the representative of that better and really respectable one whose good sense kept it in the background, which caused this regiment to be unjustly criticised and hated—and by none more than its co-nine months comrades of other organizations. To show how prejudice will jump at conclusions, it was confidently predicted they would never stand fire; but they did stand fire bravely, and acted in many respects in a most creditable manner for so new an organization. A story went the rounds, and which may not be true, to this effect:—On the Tarboro expedition, the 44th were in the advance, when the cavalry, after waking up the rebs, and finding them in large force ahead, fell back, and their lieutenant (Mix), seeing no one taking the necessary steps in such an emergency, rode up to the captain of an advance company of the 44th, and said:

"Deploy your men, captain; the rebs are close upon us!"
To which the captain replied—
"I don't know how!"
"Then," replied Mix, "right about, and run like hell, or you'll be gobbled up!"

Again, at the battle of Kinston, it was said that the 44th who were laying down, were ordered to charge the rebel line, which had begun to waver and show signs of weakness; that they refused, and the 10th Connecticut (three hundred strong) were ordered up, charged upon the rebels, and, in charging, had to walk over the prostrate 44th. I give this story without vouching for its truth; for, being in another part of the field, I had not an opportunity of witnessing the inception of the charge referred to, though, arriving with our regiment near the bridge by the flank ahead of the main charging column, I had an opportunity of seeing the 44th come up at the double-quick close on the heels of the flying rebels. But the story was told, and told, too, on the battle-field.

At Whitehall, however, no envious tongue could say aught against the conduct of this regiment; and I can here speak of what I saw of them, and can say they acted well under the murderous fire to which they were exposed.

Another anecdote of the 44th, and I have done with them; and, lest I might be accused of harboring any of that feeling towards them I have already alluded to as prevailing in the department, and which I most heartily condemn, I will state that I do not believe one word of it, and only give it a place here to show how far human malignity and envy will make men forget what is due to self-respect and to co-laborers in a good work. During the siege of Little Washington, it was stated that the rebels sent in a flag of truce, requesting the commander of the post to send the women and children, *and the* 44*th*, to a place of safety, as they were going to assault the town.

The 5th regiment came about the same time the 44th did. They were a fine, hardy-looking set of men, and participated with credit in all the expeditions undertaken during their term of service in this portion of the department.

The 45th regiment was the next—a fine body of men; but they, too, like the 44th seemed to assume too much importance, and came in for their share of ill-will; but, speaking from my own knowledge, I never knew of but one instance in their whole career where they did not seem to be up to the mark, and this time from no fault of the rank and file. The fault, if any, lay with the officers. I allude to a little affair at a place called Cole Creek, on the railroad towards Kinston, in May '63, where, by the Colonel of the 45th outranking our Lt. Col., the regiment had the advance, and when it came in sight of an earthwork manned by a few rebs, the Colonel anxious for his men, and not wishing to be precipitate, seemed to hesitate. Colonel Fellows riding up, asked him why he did not advance on the enemy's work, replied that he thought it too strong.

"Allow me," said Colonel Fellows, "and I will take it with my two flank companies."

The consent was obtained, and companies A and F of the 17th walked into the works, which had been hastily abandoned on their approach by the rebels. As I said before, this result was no fault of the rank and file of the 45th, whom I have seen marching in under fire, with ranks precisely dressed up, and acting with coolness and intrepidity.

The 43d seemed the favorite regiment with the three-years men, who regarded it as the best of the nine months men. They were, indeed, a fine lot of men, and, I have no doubt, if circumstances placed them in the post of danger, they would prove themselves fully as reliable as the three-years troops. In saying this, it will, of course, be inferred, that I do not consider the nine-months men as reliable in an emergency as the three-years men ; and, I do not think them so, generally speaking—not because the men are inferior in regard to courage or endurance; but because they are not really soldiers but militia, and not so self-reliant as the three-years men.

Of the other nine months men I know but little, save that they were a fine lot of men, and if they did not do anything to distinguish themselves, it was no fault of theirs, but because they lacked the opportunity.

A few words in regard to the feeling of the three-years men towards the nine-months troops. The men of the old regiments, almost to a man (but there were some exceptions) seemed to regard them with a feeling of envy and dislike, and the frequent salutations of 'how are you, three hundred dollars and a bugle?' partly showed from whence the dislike came. I say partly, for the other reason was, that, besides receiving so high a bounty, they could return at the end of their time of service,—which to men who had already served eighteen months, and still had a year and a half to serve, seemed unfair. And certainly, looking at the matter with their eyes, the thing did not seem altogether right, though it might very properly be argued that as the three-years men went into the service with their eyes open, and agreeing to the terms of the Government, they had no right to complain.

## PART II.

EXPEDITION TO GOLDSBORO—SKIRMISHING—SOUTHWEST CREEK—BATTLES OF KINSTON, WHITEHALL, AND GOLDSBORO—INCIDENTS—RETURN OF THE EXPEDITION TO NEWBERN—THE 17TH RELIEVED BY THE 45TH IN NEWBERN—ACROSS THE TRENT—BUILDING FORTS—SICKNESS—BEAUFORT—AN ACCOUNT OF THE FREEDMEN, ETC., ETC.

The indulgent reader, who has accompanied me thus far in my perigrinations through Dixie, need not be alarmed, upon looking at the caption of this page, at the prospect of being bored with so many dry, solid pages as he has waded through in the first part of this work. I have prepared this literary feast, if not of the best materials (and I have no better, I assure you), at least after the most approved style of French cookery, and, therefore, have kept back the best dishes to the last. It is in this second part of my humble work, that I hope to give the most stirring (I might say thrilling) and interesting part of my narrative of

"Moving accidents by flood and field,"—

and, if I do not succeed to my own satisfaction, I hope, at least, to give satisfaction to my patrons. This done, I can pocket the profits with a clear conscience.

In November, 1862, when the nine-months troops had about all arrived, the work of brigading them with the old regiments, and drilling them in field movements, was undertaken and vigorously prosecuted.

Preparations on a scale of considerable magnitude for a large expedition had been going on for some time; but to what point it was destined was wisely kept a secret, though it was generally understood to have some connection with the movement of Burnside in Virginia.

On the 8th of December, the war-worn veterans of General Wessel's brigade (of Gen. Peck's division) arrived in Newbern, and preparations for the expedition were hastily completed. The same evening, at dress parade, an order was read from Gen. Foster to all the regiments, to be ready to march in thirty-six hours in light marching order, viz.: without knapsacks, carrying only blankets and overcoats, with three days cooked rations to be carried in haversacks, seven days' to be conveyed in wagons.

The following day was a busy one for the quartermasters of the Subsistence Department, and the cooks. In the evening the guards were withdrawn, and the 8th Mass. regiment, which had not yet been fully provided with arms and equipments, took charge of the city, and sent out details of men to patrol the streets.

This was a busy night for us all. Like sailors before a storm, we had to make snug our tackle, and spread only as much sail as we thought the ship could conveniently carry. Everything in the shape of spare clothes and blankets were snugly packed in our knapsacks; and, when the final order came for us to be in line at three o'clock in the morning, we were ready at the moment to start. But we visited Billy Patterson, and each man proceeded to stow away into his haversack what he judged would be sufficient to subsist him for three days. We then turned in, to gain a little repose and freshen our energies against the morrow.

At three o'clock on the morning of Thursday, Dec. 11, 1862, we were awakened by the bugle call, and after a hasty meal, formed in the yard of our quarters, and proceeded to the place of rendezvous for the regiment on —— street. A gray, frosty mist enveloped the city, which was alive with marching men, horse, foot, and artillery, and forage and ambulance trains. As early as was the hour, however, the whole population—especially the negro portion—seemed abroad in the streets, and many a fervent prayer and good wish for our success were showered upon us by the poor negro women as we passed along.

"Oh," exclaimed one, "I know de Lord am walkin' alongside ob you, and you will beat de rebs, I knows—I knows!"

"Aunty," sang out a soldier from the ranks, "if I don't come back you'll never get paid for them clothes you washed for me."

"Nebber mind de close, honey," exclaimed the generous old woman; and then, changing her tone, she continued, as if to herself—"Oh, Lord!—de Lord!—Oh good Lord!—Nebber come back!—Oh, de poor sojer!—Lord, help de poor sojer! Amen for de poor sojer!—Amen! Glory!"

We halted on the Trent road, just beyond Fort Totten, and awaited the movement of the various bodies of troops that were to precede us.

The morning broke clear and cool, and beheld a fine array of infantry, cavalry, and artillery taking up their line of march by the Trent road from Newbern. The sight was magnificent as the long lines of infantry with their polished arms, and the cavalry and artillery, slowly but cheerfully took up their line of march, with an elasticity of step and a merry hum of voices that unmistakeably showed how high the spirits and expectations of all were aroused, and that it required only an able general to lead such an army on from victory to victory.

As we advanced into the country the evidences of former strife everywhere met the eye, in the desolated plantations, houses burned to the ground or partially destroyed, and an air of ruin and desolation pervading all.

After a tedious, plodding and plunging march of about fourteen miles, the army bivouacked for the night on a plantation which seemed more fortunate than many others we passed. But its time had come; and as regiment after regiment arrived and stacked arms, it was a curious study to watch the rush they made for the nearest fence, the eager scramble for rails, and the disappearance of the fences, as if by magic. As night darkened over the scene, the countless bivouac fires rose in all directions, casting a lurid glare up to the sky, and forming about as picturesque a scene as could possibly be imagined. And the sound of voices and laughter, and the neighing of horses and unearthly braying of mules, all combined to render that (my first) bivouac a something to be remembered forever.

Beyond where we encamped Thursday evening, the rebels having notice of our approach, blockaded the road for two miles, by felling trees across; but the pioneers set about removing them during the night, and when the army resumed its march in the morning the way was cleared, and we passed on 'into the bowels of the land.'

About 10 A.M., on Friday, a skirmish occurred near Trenton, between our advanced guard of cavalry and some rebel cavalry and infantry, in which the latter were routed with the loss of three or four killed and several wounded and taken prisoners.

Our advance reached Southwest Creek about noon on Saturday, and the enemy, about 2,000 strong, were posted beyond, with a battery commanding the road.

The 9th New Jersey and Morrison's battery were sent forward to feel their position, and a smart cannonade of some two hours' duration took place, when the 9th New Jersey made a detour through the woods and captured the battery, putting the rebels to flight. They made another stand about four miles this side of Kinston, when the same force pushed after them and engaged them for about half an hour, when the rebels again fell back.

While the skirmish was going on, the troops, as they arrived, were assigned their places in line of battle, almost parallel with the road. Towards evening, the regiments bivouacked in the same position they had taken when expecting the assault of the enemy. We were pretty hungry by this time, you may depend, not having, some of us, tasted food for nearly two days. When orders were given to stack arms, there was a general rush for rails, but some of the boys, while seeking out the latter, came across some luckless porkers, which bit the dust, were skinned, and their still quivering flesh subjected to a barely warming process, ere it was devoured by the half-famished soldiers. I fell in for a stray piece, and computed that the flesh I was then devouring, had fifteen minutes before formed a portion of an animate pig, careless of sorrow, and only seeking some innocent pieces of garbage or succulent root wherewith to tickle his palate and satisfy the cravings of hunger. How rapid are transmutations, sometimes! Little did that pig dream that on the morrow he would stimulate the nerves of many a soldier in the defeat of rebels and the capture of Kinston. But so it was; and this curious fact might lead me, if I were given to abstract reasoning, to trace this influence of forces by the abundance of pork. But no; for me are plainer and perhaps more demonstrative revelations.

There was a house in our front about one fourth of a mile distant, whither some of our lads found their way, and soon all the available beds and bedding which the frightened inmates left behind were confiscated and appropriated by the tired soldiers. The pig did not satisfy me. I was too fond of vegetables to be satisfied with flesh, and, accordingly, set out at the first opportunity in search of sweet potatoes. Espying a house upon a rising ground, about a mile to the right of our encampment, I made for it; but night came down just as I was starting, and I was compelled, as it were, to grope my way through a rice-field or swamp that intervened, where I met many a ditch and slough, some of which I avoided, and some I fell into. But, nothing daunted, I held on, and drew near the house, when I beheld in the darkness the dim outlines of a man in my path, of what description—union soldier or guerilla, friend or foe—I could not make out. Not being in the mood to stand upon ceremony, I accosted him as I approached (he proved to be a friend), inquiring if he knew of any deposit of sweet potatoes in that region. Returning a cavalry pistol to his belt with which he had covered me on my approach, he directed me to where I could find what I desired; and it may be inferred that I was not slow in availing myself of the opportunity afforded, and soon set out on my return loaded with sweet potatoes. I had almost cleared the swamp, and was approaching the camp-guard of one of our batteries—in fact I was almost upon the guard—without being perceived, when plump! down I went into an undiscovered ditch or drain, frightening myself as well as the guard, who brought his piece down to the 'charge,' expecting he had some atrocious guerilla on hand. I soon explained matters to his satisfaction, however, and went on my way rejoicing. My success awakened the hungry ones of Co. K, and the officer in command, appreciating the necessity of the men having a good supper, sent half-a-dozen along with me to the scene of my discoveries. I was a willing guide, and we soon returned with an abundance of provisions, and made a hearty supper upon the plunder. We slept well, and awoke next (Sunday) morning refreshed, and ready for the road and the fight.

On Sunday morning the 14th, we resumed our march on Kinston. From the place where we encamped, a steep hill descended, and the road wound through a low, swampy ground for about two miles, when we came out upon higher land, where our advanced guard (the 9th New Jersey and Wessel's brigade) had bivouacked for the night. The advance was already in motion, and our regiment followed. In the low grounds of Southwest Creek, we saw the evidences of yesterday's strife— two cannon captured, and a few dead rebels. When we passed the low lands, we saw abundant evidences of hasty preparation for resisting our advance; but, I suppose, as a very considerable body of the enemy—who expected us on the other road where they were very strongly fortified—could not be got up in time, Evans thought it prudent to abandon them. We had not proceeded far, however, when the crack of musketry told us that our advance was driving in the enemy's pickets; and soon, as we shortened the distance between us and the scene of the coming battle, the more regular and deliberate volleys of small arms announced that the ball had opened in earnest. Soon the artillery came galloping up, and took position, just as we reached the wood skirting the battle field. We were halted, and ordered on to the right of the road to support a battery.

The enemy were advantageously posted in a swamp, and on a rising ground beyond, about a mile from the bridge leading across the river to Kinston.

The action, which was commenced by our advance in the morning, was sustained with vigor, until the main body of our forces came up, when the battle became more earnest and terrible, and, as battery after battery arrived in position, and opened its fire on the enemy, the ground fairly shook with their repeated reverberations, while the sharp roll of musketry— whole battalions delivering their fire at once—filled up the intervals. The rebel position was well chosen, under cover of a dense undergrowth of wood, their foreground protected by groves of pines, which, however, offered no impediment to our artillery, which mowed them down like grass.

I stated that the 17th were ordered to the right to support a battery. As we marched in to take our position, the officer in command of the battery, asked—

"What regiment is that?"

"The 17th Massachusetts," was the reply.

"All right, boys," said the officer, and turning to his men, he remarked, "I'm glad they didn't send me one of those d—d nine months regiments."

We stood a few minutes in the position we had first taken, the cannon booming away like thunder, and the bullets began to p-e-e-w athwart our line, quite lively—hurting nobody however—when the artillery officer, who was on horseback, said—

"Here they come—the devils are on us!"

We could see the flash of bayonets at the edge of the wood, and fully expected a charge. Our Colonel ordered the men to fall back a few yards to a fence, unsling their blankets, and fix bayonets. This was done in less time than it takes me to record it, and we waited with anxiety the onset of the rebels.

Here, for the first time, was I brought into a position that required courage and resolution; but though I felt determined to 'do or die,' a strange feeling came over me, and if I was not really frightened, the feeling was marvelously like fear. I suppose every man who first goes into action is troubled with a sensation something akin to that which I felt at this time; but, like every new sensation, it soon wears off, and the experience of the actual dangers of conflict serves to obliterate all such qualms, and leaves the individual in the full enjoyment of a reckless indifference to what may betide, and an implicit confidence in that fate which may be the preservation or destruction of his dear life.

While we were in position awaiting the onset of the enemy, an incident occurred, which showed how serene men will look upon others going into the same danger they are in themselves.

A negro teamster, with his ammunition cart, was ordered further on, to supply another battery on our right whose caissons were running low of ammunition. The poor fellow thought he was going to his death, and if ever mortal fear displayed itself upon the countenance of any human being, it was upon that poor darky's face. I shall never forget the wild rolling of his eyes, nor the frenzied and agonized expression of his face, as he hesitatingly guided his team in front of our regiment, urged on by our men with such encouraging remarks as—

"Go it nig; don't be afraid!" "You're a goner, old darky,—good bye!" "Won't the rebs chaw him up?" &c.

We waited some time for the rebels to appear, but they came not. In the meantime, the battery we were supporting was ripping up the woods in front in fine style—at every discharge cracking off the pine trees as if they had been pipe stems.

At length an order came for us to proceed further down to the right, where the 9th New Jersey and a battery had preceded us, and here we crossed a swamp, and turned the enemy's right.

We were to push on; but our Lt. Colonel, not, perhaps, understanding the order fully, halted us in a cleared field beyond the swamp, and ordered us to lay down. The 9th New Jersey were off in the woods to our right, and when I first beheld them I took them for rebels. From the position occupied, we could see the long line of intrenchments in our front; but we did not suppose a river intervened, which was the case. During the movements just recorded, the firing had been rapid and tremendous, and, from the cheers of our men, we could clearly infer that the rebels were giving way. Then was the golden opportunity for us—for, had we then advanced as we did afterwards, instead of taking a few hundred prisoners, we should have cap-, tured an entire brigade—but it was lost. Col. Amory coming up soon after, said—

"Why do you stay here? Forward, as quick as you can!"

The regiment rose like one man, and, on the order being given to go forward at the double quick, rushed down with a yell. As we neared the bridge, we beheld a rout—an almost indescribable body of men running for their lives. All discipline seemed lost, and casting aside guns, equipments and clothing, and, in fact, whatever might retard their flight, they fled like a herd of frightened deer, while close upon their heels came on the charging columns of our men. It was a magnificent, and yet it was a pitiable sight. As intimated before, we succeeded in bagging a goodly number; but the bridge being set on fire, we were forced to give over the pursuit until the flames were extinguished.

While laying down in the field, I observed a substantial looking two-story house in our front, and near the bridge, a large portion of the rear of which had been shattered by a shell, evidently the work of the enemy. I found this the case when we halted near the bridge, from which position I could observe that the missile had entered the roof of the piazza, went clean through the house, bursting as it was penetrating the rear wall, and making the havoc described. Standing upon the piazza, the picture of anguish and despair, were two women, who seemed watching the rout of their army with a terrible and heart-sick interest, perfectly heedless of the missiles of death flying around thick and fast. Some of our officers, taking pity upon the poor women, and solicitous lest the exposure should endanger their lives, approached, and advised them to retire to a place of safety. But they resolutely refused to stir from their dangerous position. Doubtless, they had friends near and dear to them in the fight, and anxiety for the fate of those loved ones made them forget the natural timidity of their sex, and thus risk their lives.

It has been often stated that the women of the South did more to drive the men to take up arms against the Government than the politicians. If this be so—and my experience makes me think it probable—then they have most surely reaped in the whirlwind of desolation which has burst upon their hitherto peaceful homes the most bitter fruits of the wind of treason they have sown. To them, unlike the women of the North, the fields of strife are not afar off, and they do not have to weep for their braves fallen in the distant battle-field. The clouds of strife gather and burst about their homes. They see their fields laid waste,—their towns and villages made the abode of desolation and anguish. They behold their sons, brothers, fathers, and friends stricken down by the hand of war before their eyes. Danger lurks forever at their doors. Famine—gaunt, ghastly, insatiate—forever hovers in their future, like a bird of ill omen. They are forced to many a weary struggle to provide the necessaries of life for their helpless, and too frequently, alas! fatherless children. Like the first of their sex, they incited disobedience, and now they find their paradise changed to an abode of wretchedness and misery, and are compelled, in tears and wretchedness to eat the bitter fruit of their crime. I have seen the widowed wife and orphan children standing pale, motionless and horror-struck over the dead body of the husband and father, and, with glassy eyes look upon the passing array of their foes, fierce and triumphant in the 'pomp and circumstance of war;' and I have thought what a pity that even so great an offence should have so terrible a punishment. But 'those whom the gods wish to destroy they first make mad.'

The attack on Kinston was planned and carried out by Gen. Wessel, and, though the fight was more severe, and of much longer duration than the battle of Newbern, a difficult position was carried with comparatively small loss—(about 100 killed and 400 wounded).

The rebels had chosen their position, as before stated, upon a slight elevation beyond a swamp, and on both sides of the Kinston road. Their left was protected by a church and a growth of scrub oaks, and their right by a grove of large trees, their front and both flanks being pretty well protected by a swamp, difficult to cross, and densely covered with a growth of small trees and pines.

BATTLE OF KINSTON.

The brigade of Gen. Wessells opened the ball in fine style, driving in the rebel advance, and alone sustained the onset of the rebels, until the brigades commanded by Cols. Amory, Heckman, and Stevenson got into position, when they formed the left wing of our line of battle—Stevenson and Heckman the centre, and Amory the right.

Gen. Evans commanded the rebel army, which consisted of over five brigades of about 15,000 men, including a brigade of home-guards from Raleigh. The other troops were mainly from South Carolina, Georgia and Mississippi. Evans disposed his men in a skilful manner upon and behind the rising ground he had chosen for the battle-field, and had several batteries so disposed as to command the approaches by the road in front, and his left flank, which, however, was his weak spot. The fire of the rebels upon our attacking columns was rapid and well-directed, and did great havoc among them; but our line kept steadily though slowly, from the nature of the ground, advancing upon them, and, after a severe contest of over five and a half hours, and just as the 17th and 9th New Jersey had succeeded in turning their left, an impetuous charge was made, and the day was ours.

We halted in a field, and were ordered to lay down, our left resting on the river. The few remaining rebels on the other side kept up a desultory but sharp fire upon our men and the 9th New Jersey in our front.

Orders to fire had not been given, and we had to lay quietly and forego many a good opportunity of picking off a stray rebel. But human nature could not stand such inaction always, and many a sly shot was planted upon the opposite bank, sometimes with excellent effect. I had my eye upon a rebel who kept firing from behind a tree, and seemed particularly active in picking off our men, and suddenly formed the resolve to shoot him if I possibly could. Slipping quietly to the rear, I made quick time for the left of our line on the river bank. Just as I arrived, I found one of Co. K's men, named Kendrick, in the act of firing, and on looking across to see the result of his shot, saw a huge porker jump into the air as if struck. Sam fixed that fellow's hash for him, and it afterwards became a common saying—"Who killed that pig?—Sam Kendrick." But my man, who was behind a tree, abandoned his shelter and made off just as I had got my battery into position. I fired, and, throwing up his arms, he fell forward on his face. Feeling like a prize-fighter, who had drawn his 'first blood,' I leisurely returned to my place in the ranks, reloading my piece as I went along, when I was accosted by Capt. Day, who was acting Major—

."You have been firing without orders."

"Yes, sir."

"What name?"

I told him.

"What company?"

"K."

Going along the line with me to where the company was, he ordered the officer (Lieut. Greeley) to put me under arrest.

"What will all this amount to, lieutenant?" I asked.

"Nothing," he laconically replied, "take your place in the ranks."

"What's the matter?" queried some of the men.

"Nothing," I replied, "only I've been arrested for shooting a reb."

"Is that all!"

Men were detailed, under the guidance of Major Frankle, Provost Marshal, to put out the fires which had been kindled by the retreating rebels, which, in a short time, was accomplished, and the 9th New Jersey crossed over followed by the 17th.. And here I had an opportunity of seeing some of the most terrible evidences of human strife. The bridge was actually paved with cast-off arms and equipments, while in the midst of where some of the fires had been, I beheld one of the most sickening sights that ever met my gaze. Some of the poor fellows who had been wounded by our fire on the retreat, or been trampled down by the rush of the flying host, were burnt to a cinder, and I could actually see the fat seething and boiling in the hollow of the temple of one of the charred remains.

Upon reaching the other side of the river we halted, amidst a promiscuous mass of dead, dying, and wounded men—of clothes, arms and equipments. It was here that the 9th New Jersey picked up (captured?) the battle-flag of the 22d South Carolina regiment, a magnificent silk banner, with the palmetto tree on one side of the field, and a wreath of stars on the other, and the red, white and red stripes.

A few yards from where we halted, was an abandoned field piece with its caisson, which the rebs had left behind in their flight. It was the same cannon which had fired the last rebel shot in the battle, directed at our regiment, over which it burst, and wounded two or three men. I had the curiosity to examine some of the cartridges in the caisson, and found them, as well as the fixed ammunition of the small arms used by the rebels labelled with the maker's name (which I forget) 'London, England.'

After a short halt we advanced up towards the town of Kinston, whither the 9th New Jersey had preceded us. The road wound along the river bank to the left for a short distance, and then took a turn to the right into the centre of the town. At the entrance to the town, the 9th New Jersey were halted, and when we came up mutual cheers were exchanged.

Just then Gen. Wessells came riding up at the head of his brigade of Pennsylvanians and New Yorkers. He was a fine specimen of a man, tall, straight as an arrow, and with a pleasing, and even gentle expression of countenance, that indicated a humane disposition, and these indications were not false, if the love and admiration of his men were any evidence. He seemed, by his gray hair and a few wrinkles on his noble face, to be over fifty years of age; but, otherwise, in elasticity of movement, apparent vigor, and by the keen, quick glances of his honest gray eyes, he looked much younger.

The rebels, after collecting their stores and all the cotton they could gather into a heap, set them on fire. They also set fire to the railroad depot, a handsome brick structure, but this was extinguished by our men before it had made any considerable headway.

Previous to our entering the town, a flag of truce demanding its surrender had been sent in; but as it was found the enemy had abandoned the town, a messenger was sent back acquainting Gen. Foster with the fact, the party kept on to find the skedaddlers, if possible. About two miles beyond the town they came up with Evans, who sent back word to Gen. Foster to have the women and children removed, as he was going to return the fire, which all the while had been kept up by our heavy guns upon his retreating forces. This was simply a ruse to gain time; for, after our forces had been brought up and disposed in line of battle, and the cavalry and skirmishers had advanced up to where they expected to find the enemy, it was ascertained the bird had flown.

Our regiment, which had been detailed from the brigade, and when we entered Kinston was ordered on provost duty, in view of the anticipated fight, was ordered to rejoin the brigade; but, when the skedaddle was discovered, we were again assigned to provost duty, and such marching and countermarching, and shifting, and looking around for a vacant place to serve as quarters for the night, as the men of Co. K had, never fell to the lot of so tired and hungry a set of men to experience. I suppose some of the other companies could boast of a similar experience.

But do not suppose the men of the 17th were satisfied with only one job on hand at a time. No, sir. They could do provost duty; but they could also, when hungry, find something to eat (and drink) if such were comeatable. In this instance the way poultry suffered was a caution; and there was something truly ludicrous, too, in the exhibition of men gravely marching in the ranks, each having in his hand a couple of hens, or a turkey, or a goose, all of which made such a noise and flutter that it was next to impossible to hear the word of command when spoken.

The Major (Frankle), who, as a general thing, was very severe in his denunciations of such proceedings, replied to a woman, who complained that she had lost all her fowl:

"Vat—all your shickens gone? You may be tankful it was no more! If you did not have more to eat than my men, and march and fight so hard, I tink you would take a little shicken, too!"

The town of Kinston is one of the neatest and most tidy-looking I have seen in North Carolina, or, in fact, elsewhere. It is finely laid out, in a splendid location upon the banks of the river, the streets running at right angles; the houses well built, painted white, and to each is attached a beautiful and tasteful flower garden. The jail was a small but solid-looking structure, and empty. A church, small, but with a high steeple, (the top of which had been struck and bent by a cannon-shot), stood in the centre, and an air of so much quiet and comfort—so different from anything we had seen in Dixie, and so unexpected in this place—pervaded it, that the men of the 17th incontinently fell in love with the place, and wished for nothing better than to do provost duty in Kinston forever.

We had not been long in the town when mines of apple-jack, peach brandy, and tobacco were discovered, and the various expedients resorted to by the men to get at the same were as amusing as they were generally successful. People who left their houses with clothing and other matters behind, must have found a considerable change when they came back. Indeed, some of them returned during our occupation, and a more pitiable sight could not well be imagined, than those small processions of timid women and helpless children who came flocking back to their homes upon being assured of protection.

Apple-jack and peach brandy, which had been discovered somewhere by the most expert foragers, soon made their influence felt, and incited the soldiers to committing many curious pranks. Here would be seen a burly soldier, with a woman's dress, even to the bonnet, put on over his own, his musket still on his shoulder, and linked arm in arm with another soldier, presenting as grotesque an appearance as could well be imagined—while in another place could be seen a party intently engaged in harnessing a diminutive mule to a vehicle, the quadruped resenting such freedom as only a mule can.

A cavalryman passed us, with a bucket in each hand, urging his horse to its utmost speed, and shouting as he went on—

"Plenty of rum, boys!—lashins!—lashins!"

The inhabitants (those who remained) looked glum and chopfallen enough; but the negroes—it seemed a gala day to them, especially the juvenile portion, who ran around among 'de sojers' as if they were friends returning after a long absence.

"How is you, Yankees? I's glad you'm come!" was the general salutation; and the negro women vied with each other in emptying their larders to give 'de sojers suffen good.'

Towards night (having, like Ishmaelites, wandered about all the evening in search of quarters) we obtained an entrance into a hardware and furniture store; but just as we were going in an order came, directing us to guard the prisoners. We proceeded to the upper end of the town, near the depot, and there took charge of a squad of about 400 rebels, and escorted them to a large unoccupied building at the other end of the town. On our way thither, I had an opportunity of speaking with several of them. Although they differed in some things, yet they all seemed to agree in one thing, viz., in being heartily sick of the war, and desirous of peace.

Observing among them a man in Quaker's garb, I remarked—

"Friend, you do not look like a fighting man. How did you get here?"

To which he replied, in a half-crying tone—

"Thou art right, friend. I am no fighting man. I never fought in my life! I don't want to fight—I won't fight! Thy horsemen caught me on the road, and thee seest the result."

Observing an elderly gentleman in civilians' clothes, I remarked—

"You do not look like a soldier either, friend?"

"No, sir," he replied, "I'm not a soldier; nor would my conscience allow me to fight in the confederate cause. I've always been a Union man, and am so still."

I cautioned him about expressing sentiments that might compromise him when we left, as it was not certain how long he would receive protection from our arms; but he replied, that he cared not; his sentiments were already well known, and while he lived he would express them to friend or foe.

Observing he was lightly clad, I asked if he had any friends in the city who could supply him with clothes and something to eat. He said his son-in-law, named Patterson, lived just across the street, and would attend to his wants, if acquainted with his situation. I offered to carry a message to Mr. Patterson, who expressed surprise at his father-in-law's arrest, saying he was one of the few men in that neighborhood, who had all along remained true to the old flag.

He immediately repaired to the provost marshal's office, and, I had the satisfaction of knowing, was successful in obtaining the old gentleman's unconditional release.

We left our blankets and overcoats on the field, and the night being cold, after our blood had cooled somewhat, when the day's excitement was ended, we felt the need of some covering, and a party of our company was made up to go over and get them; but we could not procure a team, and the project was abandoned. I, however, had no notion of doing without my overcoat, and, with two or three others, who were of the same mind, started for the field. We passed over the place where the fighting had been thickest, and stumbled upon, and over, evidences of the deadly strife—inanimate bodies of friend and foe, maimed and disfigured. But I will not dwell upon the sickening scene revealed to us by the light of the camp fires; suffice it to say, that we were successful in obtaining our clothing and returned to our temporary quarters tired and hungry.

During our absence, a hotel had been set on fire, whether by design or through accident, could not be found out. It was burning fiercely when we returned; and, despite the efforts of our men to extinguish it, was destroyed, together with some small dwellings adjacent.

The gunboats had come up to a blockade about four miles below the city, which was commanded by an earthwork fort; and, after we had driven the rebels out of Kinston, we could hear the continuous boom of heavy artillery in that direction. A squad of the 3d New York Cavalry started for the scene, and surprised and captured the fort that was pounding away at the gunboats, and nearly all in it.

The result of our day's work may be summed up in a few words—we beat the rebels from a strong position, took over 500 prisoners, and 11 pieces of artillery.

The battle of Kinston was won on the same day on which the battle of Fredericksburg was fought.

On Monday morning we were awakened early, and with the 9th New Jersey, took up the advance. Recrossing the bridge, we passed over the battle-field, and here I observed a fine mastiff laying down beside the body of his dead rebel master. I had often read of such things; but I had at last the privilege of seeing for myself that noble instinct of affection which binds so closely the ties between man and the inferior animals.

About two miles on the road to Whitehall (for we had turned off in that direction), I left the ranks, and went into a house at the road-side. A poor widow, with three or four young children, constituted the family. The poor woman seemed terribly frightened, and in a tremulous voice told me her husband had been in the rebel army, and had died at Manasses; that she had to depend for her support, and that of her children, upon the labor of the loom, and that the house she lived in was given her for occupation, free, by a gentleman who owned the plantation on which it stood. She gave me some corn-bread, and I gave her in exchange a few biscuit and some tobacco, for she smoked; and with pity in my heart for the poor woman and her helpless family, I left them, none the worse off for my visit, and rejoined the regiment which had halted for a rest a short distance ahead.

About mid-day, however, I began to feel my legs growing stiff, and being unable to keep up with the regiment, I 'fell out' and straggled—for the first time. Charles Renaud (our late cook, whom I have mentioned before) was in the same boat, and we soon came together, and together trudged on as best we could, rested together, made our coffee together, and together visited many points of interest and attraction on our route, gathering a stray honeycomb here, and a stray piece of corn bread there; but the grand object of our search (which was anything of a spirituous or malt nature we could get hold of—whiskey preferred) could not be found. At length, shortly after mid-day, we came in sight of a really handsome one-story cottage house, evidently the abode of wealth and refinement, and thither we went, but only to find that we had been anticipated; the house deserted by all save a negro, and every thing in the most delightful confusion—drawers pulled out, and their contents scattered about, chairs and furniture broken, and every portable thing of value missing. But we were not disappointed at this, as our object was not plunder, but—whiskey. Bringing the point of my bayonet in close proximity to the darkey's breast, I conjured him as he wished for the success of the North, and his own freedom and life, to tell me if he had any whiskey or apple-jack stowed away about the premises. He turned pale (that is, for a darkey), his knees smote together, and, with an agonizing appeal to spare his life (which was perfectly unnecessary, inasmuch as I had no notion of confiscating it) and solemn assurances that there was nothing of the kind on the premises, directed me to a distillery, which, he averred, lay in from the road about 'haaf' a mile, on the right hand, just after crossing the second branch. Off we started, and on our way questioned a farmer, who, with horse and team, was requested to accompany the army so that he should not give information to his rebel friends of its whereabouts—Foster having given them the slip—but he stoutly denied all knowledge of its whereabouts, averring that there was nothing of the kind within twenty miles. Somewhat staggered by this information, we were about giving up the search; but depending more upon the darky's word than that of Mr. Secesh, we finally concluded to give the place a trial. We struck off at the point indicated, and followed a rough cart-road, which, a short distance onward, diverged into numerous roads and bridle-paths, to choose between which was no little difficulty. At length we pitched upon one, and having disencumbered ourselves of blankets, overcoats, and haversacks, which we secreted behind a fallen tree, set forward, determined to see the end of that road, at the same time keeping a wary eye in case we should stumble upon a stray guerilla party. Instead of going 'haaf' a mile, we went over two miles before we came in sight of the object of our search, which was just beyond a grist-mill, on the bank of a stream. We knew it to be a distillery by the number of casks and barrels around it, and by the peculiar odor arising from it, borne to our nostrils on the wings of the wind. But all was deserted; the mill and still-house were locked, bolted and barred, and our cautious advance found no opposition from anything animate. We paused before the strongly protected door of the distillery, and I doubted our ability to break the lock.

"Well, then, let us smash in ze door."

"But we will be heard by the guerillas who may not be far off, and what would we do if a dozen of them should come upon us?"

"Fight, I teenk."

"Fight! What chance would we have against so many?"

"We could fire, and re-treet."

"Yes; but they would probably surround us before we knew it."

"Well—dhan, I suppose we must be tak-en pree-so-neer."

"And would you like that, Charley?"

"I sup-pose if we cannot help it—what you do?" and he shrugged his shoulders.

"Are you willing to run the risk?"

"Oui—if you say so!"

But believing there might be an easier way of 'breaking and entering,' besides attacking the formidable door before us, I suggested a reconnoitre of the rear, where we found an opening defended only by a few boards nailed crosswise. These were soon ripped off, and, leaving Charley to guard against any surprise from without, I entered, taking his canteen, and proceeded to explore. There was corn in soak, and plenty of empty casks; but no whiskey. At length I lit upon a stone jug nearly full, from which came the smell of whiskey, and, giving Charley to understand I had found the prize, I proceeded to fill both the canteens, after having accomplished which, I thought it would be nothing out of the way to save what I had secured as much as possible, and therefore proceeded to fortify myself with a pull at the jug; but the first mouthful convinced me that the prize I had secured was not whiskey, but water (no doubt, the jug had contained whiskey once, as was evident from the smell). Vexed at my disappointment, I proceeded to examine further, but with no success, and I finally emerged empty-handed as I had entered. Charley was as much disappointed as I, but a shrug and muttered 'sacre' was all the evidence he gave of it. We then broke into the mill; but found nothing there except corn and some empty kegs. We went to a house or barn in the rear, filled with corn, but were equally unsuccessful. There was a house about a mile distant from the mill, and after a consultation, in which it was taken for granted that it must belong to the owner of the distillery, we started for it. Within a quarter of a mile of the house was a grove of young pines, and there we halted and arranged that I should go forward alone, and in case of danger Charley could come up at the proper, time, when I would ask him where he left the rest of the men, and he was to reply—"Waiting in the grove." Fixing on my bayonet, and looking to see if the cap of my piece was all right, I moved for the house, which I reached without molestation or discovery, except by a sentinel dog (not a fierce one), who retreated in good order at my approach. I entered the first door I came to, and proceeded through a bed room into which it opened, to the kitchen or general room of the house. My heavy tread announced a stranger, I suppose, for half a dozen females and as many children came in at once, and seemed transfixed and terrified at the apparition they beheld. Giving assurance that I intended no harm to any of them, I inquired if the master of the house was at home, and if so, where he then was? After a little hesitation, they told me he was in the garden, in front. I went out to him, and he returned my salutation without any exhibition of ill-will. I inquired if guerillas were numerous in the neighborhood, which he denied, saying, however, at length, that there had been 'a right smart' of mounted men in the neighborhood a short time previously.

At this juncture Charley came up, and I questioned, and received such answer from him as agreed upon. I inquired about the distillery, but the planter disclaimed its ownership, saying that the man who owned it, lived a 'right smart' distance beyond. Had he any whiskey? No, sir; he hadn't a drop— we might search if we pleased—he had nothing in that line but some peach brandy (spirits), which had been burnt in the distillation, but was just as good, and we were welcome to it. Taking him at his word, we poured into our canteens enough of the spirits to warrant our filling them with water, and still leave a strong drink (I didn't have the heart to take all). We then asked if he had anything to eat, as we were hungry, when his wife immediately set before us a good dish of pork, corn bread, and sweet potatoes, which we did ample justice to. The children became more familiar, and some of the youngest actually came up to us, to share in our meal. They were the finest children I had seen in North Carolina. Thanking our host— for we had nothing better to give in return—we retraced our steps in better spirits, and soon rejoined our struggling and straggling comrades, who had been, and were still, wending along on their weary way.

We had in Co. K a young fellow, of small stature, named Tom McNally, who was one of the regimental 'markers.' Tom was full of fun, and had a great love for horseflesh. He accompanied the regiment on every expedition, and it was remarked, that he always managed to have a horse to ride ('confiscated,' of course, from rebels, in a manner peculiar to Tom.) At the battle of Kinston, he came in possession of a fine colt; but, during the afternoon, while engaged in exploring the town, the animal was stolen by one of the 51st. Tom went up boldly to the headquarters of the regiment, and demanded the horse; but the colonel of the 51st told him he had no right to the animal, and should not have him.

"I've as much right to him as the other fellow," said Tom; "and if I can't get him any other way, I'll steal him back again!"

And he would have carried out his threat, but eight men of the 51st were detailed to guard the animal that night, and, of course, he stood no chance of being successful, and did not try his hand at the game.

Nothing disheartened, however, he next morning struck off ahead of the regiment, and had not proceeded above three miles before he came to a plantation, where he found a fine young mare; and actually compelled the owner to put on bridle, saddle, and assist him to mount. The wife of the planter did not wish to lose the animal, and told Tom she had a better horse in one of the fields, which he could have instead; but, suspecting the horse could not be better, he made off amid the complaints of the woman. One of the 9th New Jersey, who witnessed the affair told him it was a shame, &c.

"Shut up your head!" answered Tom, "you'd be only too glad to get a horse to ride yourself!"

And, sure enough, it was not long until Tom saw the Jerseyman mounted on a blind mule he had taken from a negro.

Shortly after, Tom procured a pair of spurs, and on applying them to the mare's flanks, developed a peculiarity, which his ready wit soon turned to account, as the following will show:

Riding up to a planter's house, he accosted a negro girl, and asked her for some eggs. She refused to give him any, when, turning the horse's heels towards her, and applying the spurs, the animal began kicking furiously, Tom at the same time exclaiming—

"If you don't get me some eggs, I'll kick your brains out!"

"O lor, massa, don't kill me, and I get de eggs!" she said, and retreated to the hen-house; but once inside, and feeling secure, she again attempted to put him off by saying there were no eggs; when, without further parley, he backed his nag up against the hen-house, and giving her the spurs, the animal commenced kicking against it so violently, that the wench, fearing the building would be knocked about her ears, piteously begged him to desist, and she would get him all the eggs he wanted. Tom drew off from the attack, and received the fruits of his victory, in the shape of a dozen eggs. The same persuasive force also procured a canteen full of peach brandy. But luck is often a fickle jade, as is a strange mare, sometimes; for, the very qualities in Tom's animal of which he was so proud, and which had served his turn so well, came near being the death of him. Passing too close to her heels one evening, the vicious brute gave him a kick in the side, and broke two of his ribs, which eventually ended in his being discharged from the regiment.

I might here pause, and give a description of the stragglers (among whom I found myself for the first time.) The mass of stragglers, as a general thing, are composed of men who become worn out with marching, or who are too footsore to keep up with their respective battalions, and fall behind, keeping on as best they can, and generally rejoining the regiments when they bivouac, though, of course, some hours after the halt for the night takes place. Some—often a great portion—of them, however, straggle for the sake of picking up stray fowls, victuals, and whatever else palatable which might fall in their way; and it was an amusing study to watch these fellows scattered and squatted along the roadside, or snugly ensconced in the angles of the fences, leisurely engaged in the work of plucking geese, turkies and other fowl, or skinning and dissecting dead porkers. Sometimes a cow would be met with and slain, and then quite a number of these stragglers would congregate, light a fire, and proceed to roast and devour the not unsavory pieces of flesh hewn from the still quivering carcase. There is, of course, a rear-guard to each brigade; but they do not succeed in keeping the men moving fast enough, and are generally compelled to 'let them slide.' Some of the stragglers, however, take a different method of prosecuting their researches, and, instead of falling behind, push ahead, and spread themselves like locusts on each flank, and generally make a clean sweep of all things eatable in their course.

The army bivouacked for the night within about five miles of Whitehall. In the morning, just before we started, a difficulty occurred between Billy Patterson and a little drummer. Words grew hot, and the drummer, making a demonstration on Billy's physiognomy, the latter (a burly, double-fisted fellow), as if resolved to die in the last ditch, exclaimed—

"Well, be——, a man has got to die but once, and I might as well die now"—

But his further utterance was stopped by the little drummer springing up and dealing him a 'sockdologer' under the ear. Before Billy could draw in his skirmishers, however, and prepare for a general engagement, an officer stepped up and separated the belligerents.

About nine o'clock on Tuesday, our advance came up with the enemy at Whitehall, who, after a sharp skirmish, retired across the river, burning the bridge behind them.

Whitehall consisted of one house, which looked as if it never knew a coat of paint, and why it was called by that name has been a mystery to me to this day. The only reasonable solution I can give to the apparent misnomer is, that a man named White, or a white man, lived there.

Upon the advance of our forces towards the river—a feint being made as if we intended to cross the same—the enemy opened on us from the opposite side with artillery and musketry. They had also a number of sharpshooters in the tree-tops, and other advantageous positions on the other bank, who kept up a continuous and pelting fire upon us, with perfect impunity, too, for we could not see them, though they could see us, and picked off many of our poor fellows.

The 17th were ordered down to the river bank on the right of the road, and got into a hornet's nest and no mistake; for the shells burst around and among us, and the bullets made the air vocal with their insinuating p-e-w-phet; but though we had quite a number wounded, not one of our number was killed.

While being actively engaged upon the river bank, our own artillery had come up, and commenced pelting at the rebs in glorious style. We had six batteries (forty-two pieces) in the

expedition, and here they were all brought into play. The enemy had also a good share of artillery, and when they all got into full working order, what with the bursting of shells and the diapason of small arms, the ground fairly shook with the reverberations.

The wooded bank of the river, in which the 17th were posted, becoming dangerous from the fire of our artillery, which ripped through the trees and drove the splinters about in all directions, wounding some of our men, Col. Amory sent in his aide with instructions for Lt. Col. Fellows to draw his men further to the rear. I was sitting cosily on the edge of a sloping bank, my legs astride the butt of a tree, and anxiously dodging my head about in search of a sharp-shooter who was, as I had occasion to believe, exclusively engaged in the endeavor to put me out of suspense and existence at the same time, when the aide came up and inquired where the Lt. Col. was. Perhaps it was officiousness on my part to direct him in the most safe and expeditious way to find Lt. Col. Fellows, who, as usual was at the front; for, without noticing my directions he preceeded further, and came near faring much worse. Just as he was taking advantage of an opening in the underbrush to go down the bank, whizz-herr-r-r-bang came a shell from the enemy which passed within two feet of him. He drew back, pale, and looking frightened enough; but, rallying, he proceeded a few yards further; but, just as he had found another opening, one of our batteries sent a discharge ripping through the woods just in front of him again, when, thinking, probably, he had gone far enough in that direction, he came to the right about, and sought the path I pointed out to him in the first place.

Our regiment was withdrawn about one hundred yards to the rear, ordered to lay down, and remained there under fire for three hours. We had, however, time to smoke, and take a survey of the battle-field on our left. The batteries were thundering away, and the regiments which were ordered in on the left of the road (among which were the 23d, 44th and 45th), were firing rapidly, and losing heavily, if one could form a judgment from the way in which the ambulance corps were carrying the wounded to the rear. Not only did the infantry suffer from the fire of the enemy, but the batteries which were most advanced suffered their share of the casualties.

A sergeant, of Belger's battery I think, was in the act of

dismounting from his horse, when a shot or shell passed through the animal, and hit the sergeant, tearing the left side completely out of him.

One of our men wishing to have a better view of some object in his front, elevated his head, and opened his mouth, when a rifle ball passed into the cavity, and out at the back of his neck, the first intimation of which we had was a stream of blood spirting out of his mouth.

Major John G. Chambers was in command of the 23d, and marched his men in under fire; then formed them in line of battle, and I could not help noticing the extreme coolness of this officer in giving the order, in a deliberate voice—

"Captains of companies, see to your allinements."

Before the engagement had any sign of abating, the 17th were ordered to take up the advance for Goldsboro. We had to pass across the battle-ground under fire every step of the way; but, strange to say, no casualties occurred during this movement. We halted opposite the house which constituted the city or town of Whitehall, when we were accosted by an enthusiastic but prudent defender of his country, who had taken shelter in the lee of the house, safe from the enemy's bullets, who exclaimed:

"I say, boys, aint we giving 'em hell?"

Bestowing upon the hero a few 'O you be d—ds,' we resumed our march, and soon left the fierce cannonade far behind us.

The battle of Whitehall was little more than an artillery-duel, and would be deserving only of a few lines of record if it occurred on the Potomac or the Rapidan. I think, in the engagement, which lasted about four and a half hours, there must have been a great deal of lead wasted and iron thrown away on our side. The only sensible impression made by our projectiles, that we could see, was upon the frame of a gunboat on the stocks at the other side of the river (intended for an ironclad), and this was certainly riddled up in fine style.

The mention of the gunboat, or frame of one, puts me in mind of a daring act performed the evening previous to the battle by one of the 3d New York cavalry. He stripped off, swam the river, and was in the act of setting the gunboat on fire, when he was discovered and fired upon, and had to dive into the river, leaving his work undone, and swim back again amid a perfect shower of bullets, not one of which, strange to relate, touched him.

The loss on our side at Whiteball was about 30 killed and 120 wounded.

Our regiment was followed by the 9th New Jersey and others, until all the infantry were under full headway, leaving only a battery and a company of cavalry to engage the attention of the enemy until nightfall.

We continued our march to within about five miles of Steep Creek, and eight of the Wilmington Railroad, and halted for the night.

On Wednesday morning our regiment, followed by the 9th New Jersey, again took up the advance, and proceeded cautiously along to within about two miles of the railroad, where, as we came out upon the brow of a hill, we could see about a mile in our front the gleaming of the enemy's arms, as they slowly withdrew. Our advance companies came up with them, and quite a lively skirmish ensued, in which Sergeant Hardy of Co. F was mortally wounded.

Lt. Col. Fellows seemed in his element, and went on even in advance of the skirmishers.

A battery had been planted on the hill just mentioned, and commenced shelling the retreating rebels.

We advanced through a wood, skirting the mill pond, and, just on the further edge of the wood, where we struck the county road, we came upon a deserted rebel camp, the fires still burning, and in the ashes of which many roasted sweet potatoes were found.

After a short halt, we advanced along the county road which crossed the railroad about a mile to the south of the railroad bridge over the Neuse river, on arriving at which place abundant evidences were manifest of a hasty preparation to receive us, abandoned in greater haste, the hoes and shovels used in making rifle-pits and breastworks being left in confusion along the track. Axes were immediately brought into requisition, the telegraph posts cut down and the wires destroyed.

We halted a few minutes just beyond the railroad, and, two companies being sent out as skirmishers to the left, took up our march on the track towards the bridge, which it was the purpose of the expedition to destroy.

This bridge was a magnificent structure, about 200 feet long, and is said to have taken twelve months to build.

The 17th had proceeded but a quarter of the distance, however, when they were opened upon by a battery placed on the track across the bridge, which, having the exact range of our position sent shot and shell into us with terrible accuracy.

The track was immediately cleared, the regiment dividing, taking each side of the railroad, (the bed of which there rose to an elevation of about ten feet,) and gradually advanced towards the bridge. The fire from the battery and sharpshooters on each side of the railroad, became so continuous and heavy that it was difficult to tell whether moving along or laying still was most dangerous; but we kept pressing on, returning the fire as best we could. Our firing was rapid, but, though the bullets flew into where the enemy were supposed to be, yet I doubt if they did much execution.

While advancing cautiously onward, and during one of those pauses in our progress rendered prudent by the iron and leaden hail directed against us, an incident occurred, which impressed me at the time as being truly ludicrous. A Co. K man, named Gately, who was hugging the side of the railroad with commendable zeal, was approached by a rebel of the canine species, which, with that instinct that often approaches to reason, and is at times wonderfully developed in this species of animal, seemed to realize that he was in the midst of danger, and sought the nearest place of shelter. For this purpose, he insinuated himself between the soldier and the ground. The man not relishing the companionship, from prudential reasons, no doubt—an inch of elevation in the position he then was affording so much of an additional mark for bullets or erratic pieces of shell,—endeavored to dislodge him, saying—

"Clear out of this, d—n you!"

But the dog would not stay repulsed, and again returned.

"Give him the butt of the musket!" suggested Phil. Mealley, (another of Co. K's men), "knock him over into the ditch!"

This suggestion was acted upon, and the dog driven off.

As we were marching down the railroad in the first place, and when the enemy opened upon us, the cry was raised among the men—Billy Patterson's stentorian voice being among the loudest—

"Unfurl the flag!"

"Let the d—d rebs see what we fight under!"

"Show them our colors!"

A man named Carney, of Co. I, who was color-sergeant, immediately responded to the call, and shook out the folds of the old 'star spangled banner;' and there he stood on the railroad track, alone, for half an hour, a mark for the enemy's sharpshooters; but, strange to relate, though two of the color guard who were lying down behind him were wounded, and the old flag riddled with bullets, he received not a scratch. This act of true bravery, no matter how ill-advised it might have been, is, I think, deserving of a record, and the honor of this deed should be given to the man who so nobly faced death while upholding his country's flag.

Having progressed in the manner described about half a mile, somebody gave the order, and every one repeated it, to form on the railroad, and charge across the bridge—what for, except to take the battery just beyond, which had so annoyed us, I could not understand. Supposing however, that everything was correct, I scrambled up the bank and took my place with the rest. Then with a shout and a cheer we commenced the charge on the double quick; but had not proceeded twenty yards when, from the skirt of woods bordering the field on our left there came—tr-r-r-r-r—a volley of musketry fired by file, followed in half a minute's time by another volley delivered at once. (I should judge from the length of the line that no less than three regiments fired each time). And then commenced a scene that it would be vain to attempt a description of, especially by an actor in it. In less time than I can relate it, every man who was not wounded, had jumped, tumbled headlong or rolled over into the ditch at the right of the track, and the regiment apparently thrown into the wildest confusion. I have been told that those who witnessed the scene thought for the moment that the 17th were cut to pieces; but were agreeably surprised to see the brave fellows spring up again, and commence a rapid fire upon the enemy, using the elevated bed of the railroad as a breastwork.

There were but four or five men wounded from these vollies. The rebels, evidently mistaking the distance (about 200 yards), and the height of the railroad bed did not fire high enough, and most of their bullets lodged in the bank at the left—an extremely lucky circumstance for us all, as was also the interruption to our progress thus given; for had we crossed the bridge few of us would ever have returned to tell the tale.

When the sound of the first volley struck my ear, I involuntarily turned my head to see where it came from, and I mentally remarked—"What splendid file-firing!" But when the second volley burst out at once, the smaller sounds uniting to swell the volume into a deafening crash, I was too absorbed in calculations upon whether any of the musical messengers of death singing about my ears, were intended for my especial misfortune, and hesitating among the confused mass of men what to do with myself, when, just as a shell burst close over me, I received a knock on the left side which doubled me up, and I toppled over, with the others, head heels into the ditch. The breath was knocked out of me, but sensibility remained; and, strange to say, while falling the short distance down the bank, I made twice over this mental calculation—

"If the bullet [I thought it was a bullet, and went quite clean through me, for I felt the pain equally in both sides] has not gone through my stomach I may get over it. If it has, I'm a goner, sure."

Picking myself up, as best I could, and, with a rueful visage, I suppose, replying to the inquiries of my comrades if I was hit, I took off my blanket, unbuckled my belt, and proceeded to search for the wound. I will freely acknowledge, that at this time my thoughts were not of the most lively character; but, upon searching and finding no wound save a painful bruise, I could have jumped for joy, and felt better pleased than if I had come into possession of the best plantation in North Carolina. In picking myself up after the tumble just described, I noticed the 9th New Jersey, who had advanced down the field to our right, retire on the order at the double-quick. And yet, afterwards, in Gen. Foster's report, this regiment received all the credit for what the 17th had done.

After a while Morrison's battery came thundering along, and got into position in the field at the right of the railroad, and commenced hurling shot and shell into the enemy in fine style.

The men were loading and firing away in splendid fashion, though I think with questionable results, and, catching the spirit of the occasion, I added my feeble quota to their efforts.

At one time, after discharging my piece over the railroad, and coming down to reload—the shot and shell of the enemy screaming and bursting over and around us, they having brought a number of their batteries to bear upon our particular position—I beheld one of our men (a very young fellow), with his head punched into the bank; and looking the picture of be-

wilderment and terror. Seeing that he appeared unhurt, I questioned him while loading my piece:

"What's the matter? Why don't you fire?" [No answer.]
"Is your piece loaded?" "Yes."
"Then, d—n you, get up, and act like a man!"

But he was too terrified to move, and I left him in disgust, although pitying the infirmity that should have deterred him from ever entering the army.

I have omitted to state that half a dozen of the marines, whom we had been guarding, had volunteered into Co. I (our smallest company in point of numbers), and in this engagement they acted with great gallantry. Our men were crowding the embankment towards the bridge, and one of the marines anxious to have his share of the fun, sung out—

"Make room for a marine, there, will you?"

"Bully for the marine!" shouted the boys, as they made way for him.

One of our fellows had taken shelter behind a log, and a non-commissioned officer observing the act, routed him out, tell- him to go forward and do his duty. The man departed, and the officer took his place, snugly ensconcing himself behind the log.

Lt. Col. Fellows was continually going up and down the line, encouraging his men, showing them by his example a pattern of the most fearless bravery.

Lieut. Graham, of the Artillery, went forward with combustibles to fire the bridge, but soon returned pell-mell, jumping behind a log, exclaiming—

"D—n them, they won't give a fellow the ghost of a chance out there!"

An order then came to form into line, and I thought it a case of particular hardship in taking up my place in the ranks to have to stand upon a log, which elevated me about two feet above my comrades, and thereby exposed me more to the flying shot and shell of our own batteries, as well as those of the enemy; for our own shells were bursting just over us, and Morrison's battery was belching forth its destructive missiles just above our heads.

The order was given, and we marched out from behind the embankment, and were halted in the rear of Morrison's battery, and ordered to lie down in a hollow made by taking earth for the bed of the railroad. The rebels seemed to have the exact range of the position, and the way the shell and solid shot scattered and tore up the earth about us, and in our midst, was a caution. Col. Fellows alone stood, and some of the officers were remonstrating with him upon the rashness of thus exposing himself, when a shell at that moment came screaming by, apparently within a few feet of his head—

"Phew! there she goes!" exclaimed Col. Fellows; and replying to the officers, he said—"Well, it appears to me, that it is just as safe standing here, as lying down; if a man is to be hit, he'll be hit lying down as well as in any other position!"

"Poor philosophy, Colonel," I thought, "but very inspiriting words."

Lieut. Barnabas F. Mann then came forward, with a bundle of prepared combustibles in his hands, and called for two volunteers to accompany him to the bridge, to operate with another party in an endeavor to fire the same. The men were instantly forthcoming, of course, and the trio started on their dangerous errand. We watched them with anxiety, and saw them gain the bridge amid a perfect death-shower of bullets, one of which, unfortunately, hit our brave Lieut. Mann on the plate of his belt, causing a severe contused wound. They returned with the wounded officer, reporting that they did not succeed in their enterprise; but were mistaken, as will be seen presently.

Faint cheers were now heard from the rebels, and on looking to ascertain the cause, it was discovered that a train had arrived with reinforcements, which could be seen rapidly defiling from the cars and forming in line of battle across the railroad. Capt. Morrison learning this, immediately jumped upon the railroad, and directed the fire of his battery. The first shell fired fell rather to the left of the rebel line. The second fell in their midst almost on the railroad track, and the way they scattered into the woods was amusing.

A 'monitor' or battery came up with this train, and immediately commenced shelling us, every shell bursting directly above our heads. At the third fire from Morrison's battery, the shell exploded the engine, and a column of white smoke shot up into the air, carrying with it, no doubt, the lives of many poor rebels.

The enemy's fire began to slacken, and just as another attempt was about to be made to fire the bridge, smoke could be seen issuing from it, and soon the whole structure was wrapped in flames. The most important part of the work was accomplished.

In the meantime the work of tearing up the rails and sleepers of the railroad, and setting them on fire, was efficiently performed by the gallant 5th Mass. regiment and the New York Cavalry, the latter destroying another railroad bridge about two miles north of the great bridge; and when the fight was concluded I had time to notice the smoke of hundreds of fires, extending as far as the eye could reach on the bed of the road, indicating how completely the work of demolition had been accomplished.

Our regiment then marched out from under fire, and were received with cheers from all the other regiments that had come up to our support.

We then took up the advance on the return movement; but had not proceeded far, when we heard firing, and cheers of men, indicating that the fighting was not yet over, and soon an order reached us to halt. We were formed in line of battle, in case the forces in front would be compelled to retreat; but after a half hour's suspense in this position, were ordered again to the scene of our late labors, where we arrived in time to see the tail end of the fight, and to find we were not needed.

It appears that just after we had retired from the field, and towards sunset, the rebels having crossed the county bridge, some two or three miles above, to the number of three or four thousand, came down and charged across the railroad upon battery B, 3d New York Artillery. They formed in three lines of battle and came on with a terrible swoop intending to crush all before them.

The captain of the battery ordered his pieces to be loaded with double charge of grape and canister, and when they came within about sixty yards, sent a hail storm into their midst which mowed them down like grass, and before they could rally or fly, sent another discharge into them which threw them into such confusion that they incontinently fled, and were seen no more. The 5th Massachusetts was supporting this battery, and received great praise for its gallant behaviour. About forty prisoners were taken, and if the artillery supports had charged, no doubt many more would have been captured.

Our aid not being required, we went to the right about, and again took up the backward track; but though night had fallen on the scene, our way was not in darkness; for some of the men —stragglers, perhaps—of the advanced regiments, had amused themselves in setting the woods on fire, on each side of the road. The scene was grand. The huge pitch-pines, which had been stripped to obtain the gum, from which turpentine and rosin were made, were ignited, and burned fiercely, and lined our road on either side like flaming sentinels. The underbrush had also caught, as well as the dried leaves, and with their volume of light added, rendered our pathway as clear and distinct as if the noon-day sun poured down his burning beams. The heavy and regular tread of the marching battalions; the rumbling of the artillery and the baggage wagons and ambulances; the braying of mules; the confused hum of voices; the occasional cry of pain from the wounded men; the fierce, flaming, crackling, and cracking of the trees on fire; the occasional crashes of the falling giants of the forest; and the illuminated cloud of smoke which hung over all, made up a picture of sight and sound that, once witnessed, can never be forgotten.

I was tired, weary, bruised, and exhausted, and felt truly glad when we halted for the night, which we did in the same place we had bivouacked the night previous.

We resumed our march next morning; but I could not keep up, and arrived at the bivouac long after the regiment had stacked arms. But on emerging from the wood in full view of the encampment, I beheld a sight which was the grandest I ever witnessed. The ground rose to a considerable elevation from and on each side of the road, on both sides of which were encamped the infantry, cavalry and artillery. I could see the long lines of bivouac fires extending to the woods on either side, and the swarthy visages of the men as they moved around, or gathered about the fires, smoking and talking over the events of the day; and, what with the braying of mules and the barking of isolated and astonished dogs, there came a hum from the host that resembled the murmuring of 'many waters.' Added to this sight of magnificence the surrounding woods on fire, and the crashing of falling trees and branches, which might lead to the delusion that quite a number of small skirmishes were going on at the same time, and you will have some faint idea of the picture that met my gaze. To one unacquainted with military matters, looking upon that scene, it would appear that instead of an army of fifteen or twenty thousand men, there were at least double or treble that number encamped before him.

On our return, we were accompanied by a goodly number of escaped slaves, and any one who beheld the processions of these escaped bondmen—and they were dotted all through and along the line—men, women and children, and witnessed the patient and even cheerful manner in which they toiled along, with all they could hastily gather up in their flight, would be convinced that their love of liberty was prompted by more than an indefinite idea of the blessings of independence. I could not help occasionally smiling at the grotesque appearance of some of the females, who had, apparently, left the more useful articles of their own wardrobe, to indulge in the inevitable female taste for finery and gewgaws, by 'confiscating' and bringing off in triumph some of their late mistresses' finery. Some were apparently unmarried, and they carried the largest amount of 'plunder,' while those who had children to carry or look after, could not bring more than a few necessaries of life, and, perhaps, a bed-quilt or blanket. Some had mules or carts; but the majority were on foot. After a tedious and toilsome march of over three days, in which no enemy annoyed our flanks, front or rear, we arrived in Newbern, as 'hard' a looking set of men as probably ever entered that city before. We were thankful. however, that our toils and fighting were over for the present, at least, and enjoyed the short repose granted us, ere we resumed our duty as provost guard of Newbern.

The 17th regiment continued in the city until the 26th of January, 1863, when it was relieved by the 45th, and went into barracks near the old county bridge across the Trent river. Here the regiment was engaged in doing picket duty, and constructing earthworks under the superintendence of Major Frankle, in which latter duty they were assisted by the 43d Mass., encamped near by.

The winter wore away heavily enough, but was enlivened by occasional dancing assemblies in the different companies' quarters, each emulating the other in the taste displayed in their decoration.

On the 14th of March (the anniversary of the battle of Newbern), the enemy made an attack upon an entrenched camp of two regiments of Wessell's brigade, across the Neuse river, and at the same same time attempted to shell the city; but the gunboat Hunchback coming to the rescue, they were driven off.

The affair was a fizzle on the part of the enemy, although from a sketch of it which I have seen in one of the New York illustrated papers, the public might be led to suppose it was most sanguinary and terrible.

I omitted to mention, in the proper place, the departure on the 7th of Feb'y, '63, of an expedition composed of a portion of the 18th Army Corps and Gen..Peck's Division of the Army of the Potomac, which arrived from Norfolk in January. This expedition, upon which so much was counted, proved a failure, owing to a disagreement between Gens. Foster and Hunter as to which general should have the chief command and direction of affairs in the operations against Charleston ; and, as Foster could not have his own way, he withdrew a considerable portion of his forces, and with them returned to North Carolina in March.

About the first of April, the rebel Generals Hill and Garnett, with about fifteen thousand troops invested Little Washington, and erected batteries so as to command the approaches by water. Gen. Foster arrived the day it was invested, and great fears were entertained for his safety as well as that of the garrison. The rebels commenced a vigorous bombardment of the position, but after fifteen days pounding, and being pounded in turn, they fell back, and raised the siege. During all this time we could distinctly hear the sound of the cannonade, although the scene of conflict was fifteen or twenty miles distant.

On the 7th of April, the 17th formed part of an expedition undertaken for the relief of the besieged city; but upon approaching a place called Blounts' Mills, the enemy was discovered in force strongly entrenched. A severe skirmish ensued, the 17th losing seven men and an officer wounded, when the position being found too strong, the troops were withdrawn, and the expedition returned, without having accomplished anything. The expedition renewed its attempt on the 17th of April, and reached Washington on the 22d, without opposition, the enemy having previously withdrawn.

On the 27th, the 17th with the other regiments of the brigade, including the 45th Mass., started on an expedition to Green Swamp, upon the railroad leading to Kinston. On the 28th, at a place called Sandy Ride, near Cove or Cole Creek, the enemy were encountered, and the 45th advanced towards where they were entrenched, and would, no doubt have driven them out in fine style, for the 45th was really a good fighting regiment, but the Col. (Codman) hesitated, not from fear, I think, but ill-judged prudence, when two companies of the 17th were ordered up by Lt. Col. Fellows, and marched into the enemy's works, which they found abandoned. The expedition returned to its bivouac of the night previous, amidst a drenching rain, having marched nineteen miles in nine hours.

On the 5th of July, the 17th formed part of an expedition under Gen. Heckman, and proceeded to Warsaw, where they made some important captures of rebel stores, and destroyed salt works, &c.

On the 1st of October, the 17th again assumed the provost duty of Newbern, relieving the 27th Mass., where it has, I believe, remained ever since.

The rebels had during the winter of 1863, made several feints upon Newbern, and drove in our pickets at various times, but never approached nearer the city than ten miles. During the Fall of '63, after the nine months troops had been all withdrawn from the department, their time having expired, the comparatively small garrison had been still further depleted by Gen. Butler (who succeeded Gen. Foster as department commander) for the purpose of strengthening other posts. The rebels fully aware of this, determined upon the capture of Newbern, and, during January, collected a force of 15,000 or 20,000 men at Kinston, and on the 26th, reached our outposts, which they drove in. About 114 men of the various companies of the 17th under command of Lieut. Col. Fellows, went to the assistance of the pickets at Batchelder's Creek, and on the 1st of Feb. were attacked by an overwhelming force of rebels, and lost eight officers and fifty men taken prisoners, and one killed and four wounded. Among the prisoners were Lieut. Col. Fellows, Adjutant Cheever (wounded), Capt. Lloyd (wounded), and Lieuts. B. F. Mann and Comins. But the rebs didn't get Newbern, although they captured Plymouth and its brave commander (Gen. Wessels), and the heroic garrison under his command. And after all the blood shed in the efforts to hold Little Washington, it has been abandoned to the enemy. Let us hope that the same policy will not be pursued in the case of Newbern, which is certainly one of the most important and strongly fortified posts held by our army on the coast.

I was taken sick in April, and sent down to Beaufort with thirty or forty other sick men. We took the cars at Newbern, and in about three hours were transported from the heat and dust of the interior to the cool, bracing air of the sea coast. On the way down I noticed that the country we passed through seemed little better than a continuation of swamps. We passed Havelock station, where a block-house had been erected in the midst of a swamp, and I pitied the poor fellows whose duty it would be to garrison that post during the coming warm season. Further on we came to clearing, and saw a line of breastworks behind which it was intended to dispute the advance of Burnside's forces in their march from Slocum's Creek to Newbern, but which he drove them from with little trouble. Newport Barracks, about ten miles from Morehead City, was a collection of some dozen houses, and the quarters of the cavalry and infantry pickets in that section. Carolina City was next reached, but where the city was I couldn't for the life of me make out. It was not anything like so grand a place as Newport Barracks, and I should not have known of its whereabouts but for the camp of the 23d Mass., which was said to be in the city. We next passed through Morehead City to the railroad terminus or wharf, about a mile further on. Morehead consists of one or two hotels, and forty or fifty houses and stores. A number of steamers and transports were laying at and off the railroad wharf. To the south, across the sound, I beheld Fort Macon, and anchored abreast of it and inside the sound were ships of all descriptions, from the captured blockade runner to the huge blockaders which were taking their rest and preparing to resume their dangerous duties off Wilmington, relieving in turn some other blockader. The city of Beaufort lay to the eastward, and looked much larger than it really was, and quite imposing.

While waiting for transportation, and looking at the various objects of interest around, my eye lit upon an individual (a sergeant in the — Mass.) whom I instantly recognized as having seen at Camp Cameron, whither he had been detailed to gather up recruits. But what a change had been wrought in his appearance! When I saw him at Cambridge he was full of life, spirit, confidence, and business—and drove a profitable trade there in the retail of porter, ale, &c. (under the rose, of course.) Now he looked cheerless and forlorn—utterly 'played out,' and as anxious as the most peacefully inclined rebel that 'this cruel war' should be ended. Hard marching, hard beds, hard usage, hard fighting and hard tack, had evidently left their mark upon him. And yet he was not sick—only dispirited a little.

A boat being at length in readiness we embarked, and after an hour's sail reached the Hammond Hospital at Beaufort. This hospital was in a building or series of buildings formerly known as Pender's Hotel, and was one of the most considerable and extensive of its class in Beaufort, and before the war was the summer residence of many planters and their families from the interior who made this city their watering place. The main structure was built out upon the shore, on piles, so that the tide ebbed and flowed under it, and was altogether one of the most delightful places I have seen in that section. The former owner (Pender) was among the first and most active in the secession movement in North Carolina, and, with a company of men he had raised in Beaufort, took possession of Fort Macon; but Burnside came along, and after taking Newbern, Morehead City and Beaufort, leisurely proceeded to knock him and his fellow traitors and their arrangements into a 'cocked hat,' and Pender was taken prisoner and forced to leave his fine hotel, with its plate, furniture and bedding, behind him; and the story went that the negroes, the poor whites who remained, and some of the officers of a Rhode Island regiment divided the spoils.

The city of Beaufort is well laid out and looks quite pleasant from the water; but though there are a few good dwellings and some old-fashioned stores, the houses are scattering and the sand ankle-keep in the streets. In fact, the city is built upon a bank of sand; and how the inhabitants managed to cultivate gardens was a mystery to me—but they did make gardens, and in some instances very creditable ones. The soil, however, seemed too sandy for any fruit trees but the fig, which flourished in great plenty. The majority of the people—who, I judge, never exceeded two thousand in number—seemed to live by fishing and gathering shells. Beaufort is so situated within the folds of a marsh, and the approaches to it are so intricate and shallow, that it can never become a place of any great commercial importance —Morehead City will be its successful rival in that respect.

We (that is, the sick men) were assisted to land, and, after our names were checked and our surgeons' certificates or assignments deposited, shown to our ward room; and, to tell the truth, we had no cause to complain of our new quarters, which were pleasantly situated in the main building, commanding an extensive view of the harbor and the sea beyond. The beds were really good—but to us poor devils who had known nothing of the kind since leaving home, they appeared truly luxurious. A little experience in the productions of the culinary department of the hospital, however, did not impress us so favorably with that part of the programme. The bread was often hard and mouldy, and the beef as solid as a frozen turnip and salt as Lot's wife. As for the soup, it was whispered around that it was nothing but sea water in which salt junk was boiled, and a few carpenters' shavings thrown in for vegetables—it was called 'salt-water soup.' Of fresh meat I never tasted any in the hospital, while of fish and oysters, which were in great abundance in the market, I did not have more than two meals during the four weeks I was in hospital. When we complained to our fellow patients of the fare, they told us it was much better than it had been.

A few days after our arrival we were called up to undergo examination by the hospital surgeon, Dr. Ainsworth. In answer to one of his queries, we all told him we liked our quarters very well, but complained about the poor quality of the 'grub.'

When Tom McNally (the hero of the kicking mare) came up, Dr. Ainsworth asked—

"Well—what's the matter with you, sir?"

"O nothing particular," replied Tom.

"What were you sent here for, then?"

"Why—to recruit my health, I suppose."

"Ah—I see. I think you'd better go back to your regiment. I send some others off tomorrow, and you can go with them."

"I'd just as soon go now, sir."

"No. You can't go till I send you."

"Well, for God's sake, give me something to eat while I am here!" returned Tom.

"Here," said the doctor to the clerk, "make out papers for this man, and have him sent off immediately!" Then, taking another sip from a glass on the counter beside him, which looked like whisky, he added—

"These 17th men seem hard to please. I shouldn't wonder if they boarded at the Revere House before they came into the army!"

That the hospital at Beaufort was not well conducted, I could plainly see, though to a visitor everything seemed to work well. And I was reminded of a reply made to an observation of mine to one of the patients in a general hospital at Newbern, that everything seemed favorable to the comfort and recovery of the sick—"Ah," he replied, "what you see is all very well—but there are many things you don't see!"

It was so with the Hammond Hospital at Beaufort. A pack of idle, worthless fellows, in the enjoyment of the most robust health—who should have been doing duty with their regiments in the field—were employed as clerks and orderlies, who, by a system of espionage upon the actions of the men and of persecution to all who incurred their displeasure, exercised a kind of petty tyranny which made them obnoxious but at the same time feared. These understrappers, while the patients were often deprived of some of the most common and desirable necessaries, reveled in the choicest dishes and delicacies to be obtained, including wines and preserves. This I have seen myself, and mentally contrasted it with the coarse fare of the poor patients who were forced to swallow the barely parboiled salt junk and dry bread, and the abominable milkless and unsweetened slops dignified with the name of tea or coffee.

And yet there was one man in authority, who seemed to do all in his power to remedy the too palpable evils. This was the assistant surgeon, Dr. Vaughan—a New Yorker, I believe. He was a kind, humane man—and to his exertions were due, in a great measure, the reforms that had been made in affairs. I have seen him day after day in the kitchen enforcing a reform in its arrangements; and I noticed, too, that on such occasions our meals were so much better than usual as to elicit remarks of satisfaction from the partakers.

'Red tape,' I presume, is indispensable in the conduct of all affairs pertaining to Government; but no where does its knotted folds tighten with more deadly effects around the destiny of its victims than in the hospitals. Hundreds die in the hospitals every year, who, if transferred to their homes at the North, might recover—if not, they would at least have the consolation of dying among their friends, which is the least that might be accorded by the Government to the poor fellows who become disabled in its service; but as they can not be sent North without a discharge from the service, and often while the discharge papers are passing through the tedious proeesses of signature ('the mill of the gods grinds slowly') the unfortunate patient becomes impatient, fretful and gloomy at the delay, and that 'hope deferred which maketh the heart sick' in many cases increases the virulence of the disease or brings on a relapse—and the poor fellow, so lately warmed with the pleasing hope of seeing once more his friends and his home, closes forever in blank despair his eyes in the bitterness of death.

[Since the above was written, I find that, through the efforts of Governors of different States and other good men in power, this evil has been partially remedied. I would respectfully but earnestly call the attention of those in power—and especially our good Governor of Massachusetts, who has always been the soldier's friend—to the adoption of some system whereby all sick men who will bear transportation can be sent home to their friends, and by this means thousands of lives may be saved.]

I will instance a case in point, to show the fatal effects of delay in the matter of discharges of sick men. A young man, named Palmer, who belonged to a New York regiment, was sent to the hospital at Beaufort, very sick from chronic dysentery.

It was thought by the surgeons, after they had treated his case for a while, that nothing could save his life but a change to a more northern climate; but this could not be effected without a discharge. They interested themselves, however, and the discharge papers were forthcoming in an unusually short space of time. The poor fellow, buoyed with the hope of again seeing his friends, rallied a little, and actually gained considerably in strength; but just as he had got on board the boat at the wharf, which was take him with a squad of other discharged men to the steamer in waiting, an order came from the surgeon that he must return, as there was some informality in his papers, and a new set would have to be made out. The poor fellow returned; but the shock occasioned by the disappointment was too much for his enfeebled constitution to bear. A relapse ensued, and in a few days he was a corpse—the victim of 'red tape,' or incompetency, or criminal carelessness—which?

I have said the undstrappers at the hospital made a 'good thing' out of the necessities of the patients. They did more. The whisky intended for hospital uses was not only used by them, but frequently disposed of to the man-'o-war's men, who paid liberally for the same. The loss to the hospital (or rather the patients) was made up in this wise: When a pail-full of whisky was drawn from the cask, it was said that an equal quantity of water was thrown in—so that when the cask got pretty well down from the withdrawal of the legitimate supplies for hospital use, it was remarked by the patients that they got water diluted with whisky, instead of whisky weakened with water as in the earlier stages of this peculiar process.

There were many other things in the management of this hospital open to criticism—though, doubtless, the fault did not always lay at the door of the surgeon in charge. For example —there was quite a large number of disabled men, whose discharge papers had been made out and sent to headquarters for signature, but had been kept back two, three, and even six months—for no reason whatever save some contemptible quibble or pretense that these papers were not made out correctly. Here were a large number of men unfit for any duty—some of them permanently disabled, others in the last stages of decline, and all anxious to be sent home as soon as possible, since they could be of no further use to and only a burthen upon the Government—kept against their own wishes, at a heavy public expense, and all because Dr. So-and-so, or Medical Director Bobolink, or their understrappers, were too indolent or careless to do their duty properly. Many of the nine-months men who had become disabled and were placed in the hospitals for discharge, were retained for some time after their regiments had been mustered out of service. No doubt it is a good and a very charitable thing to retain disabled men in hospitals whose discharge therefrom would throw them upon the charity of the world; but cases of this kind are very rare. Nearly all have friends who would willingly care for them, or belong to communities who have providently considered such contingent demands upon their charity, and made liberal arrangements to that end. In any case, I believe the condition of such men would be eminently improved by a transfer to the North—either to their friends or to some convalescent hospital or home for disabled soldiers.

I have now drawn towards the close of my narrative, and find that, instead of having room left for an elaborate essay (were I capable of writing one) upon the condition, character and habits of the freedmen, I have only space for a few general remarks. I do not regret this, however, when I reflect that there are many others better qualified for such a task than me.

In the course of my experience with the contrabands, I have been favorably impressed with their capacity for becoming a free people. The negroes seem, as a general thing, to possess a superior vitality to the white men of the South; for, with comparatively poor domestic arrangements and an inferior style of nutriment, they seem to thrive better and be capable of greater endurance and more continued physical exertion. They display a thirst for knowledge—a desire for information—an indomitable faculty of acquisitiveness, and a superior power of imitation, which must lead the social philosopher to but one conclusion, viz., their eminent fitness for advancement in the social scale from the position of bondmen to that of freemen. And the necessity of some such change in the social condition of the negroes of the South cannot but be too apparent to every fair-minded man who has beheld the universal manifestations of the desire for freedom displayed by them. They are endowed with a temperament at once docile and energetic, light and serious. They have considerable aptitude for the mechanic arts, and are probably, some of them, the best practical farmers of the South. They are generally moral and deeply impressed with the sacredness of religion; but it is true at the same time that they have many petty vices—and the wonder is, that under so debasing a system they have any virtues at all. Of the length, breadth and depth of their mental capacity I do not pretend to judge—all white men are not equal in that respect; and I trust I am not one of those who believe that nothing good can come out of Nazareth. As to the radical mental and physical difference which is said to exist between the black and the mulatto, I must confess I could never perceive it—there are the weak, puny and imbecile of both shades of color, at well as the strong and active, intelligent and energetic.

It cannot be denied that, above all other things, the negroes have an unbounded desire for freedom—extravagant only in the risks it will cause them to run to obtain that boon; for, once free, they are content—nay, happy—to begin on the most humble scale to climb the ladder of fortune. They are very domestic in their habits, and where they can find no habitation ready for them when they come into our lines, will set to work, and with such materials as very few white men would make available, erect a hut—not an elaborate one, to be sure, but all sufficient for their humble wants.

In and around Newbern I should judge there were from 5,000 to 8,000 escaped slaves, and of that number at least one half were located in camps or collections of huts of their own construction in different localities adjacent. There was one of those on the left of the Trent road, near Fort Totten; another near Fort Spinola on the other side of the Trent river, and a third just across the railroad bridge and to the left of the railroad.

This latter village, inhabited by over one thousand negroes of all ages and sexes, was under the supervision of Mr. G. R. Kimball, of Nashua, N.H. (Mr. K. was formerly Sutler of the 17th.) Upon expressing a desire to learn some facts in regard to the negroes under his charge, he kindly offered to give me all the in his possession.

The adult negroes under Mr. Kimball's charge were all in the employ of the Government—the females were engaged in cooking, washing, and making pies and sweetmeats, for which they found a ready sale among the soldiers. "And a more contented and happy lot of mortals," said Mr. K., "you can not find anywhere." This I verified from a personal inspection.

Among other places I visited the village school. It was kept by a negro named Mack Bourne, and contained twenty-five pupils. When I entered, Mack did not seem pleased at the intrusion, and said—

"Look here, sojer—I dusent want any body in de sojer business to come in here; for d'oder day one of you sojer men—he cum'd in here, and he stole a testament from me—he did—a bran new one, too—and I don't like sich work—I don't!"

I told him I did not come to take anything from him.

"What did you cum for, den?"

"My dear sir," I replied, in a melo-dramatic tone, "I am a member of the press, and take an interest in your welfare."

"You is—you do? De press—wha-what press—de ex-press?"

"No—the printing press—for printing newspapers."

"Oh!—Is you a-gwine to print a paper? I tought you was a sojer!"

"And so I am, my friend; but I'm a printer also."

"Dus you make books like dis-a-one?" displaying a primer.

"Yes; I could print a book like that, or—a testament."

"Look here, sojer," he said, the remembrance of the loss he had sustained making him suspicious.—"I tink you'm foolin' me. Now, sar, I dusent like to be fooled—I dusent!"

But I assured him I didn't want to fool him, and so pacified him that he became confidential, and told me his history. He was 'raised' in Plymouth, and had been taught to read by a nephew of his master's, who gave him lessons on Sundays, on the sly. None of his scholars had advanced beyond lessons in spelling, and most of them were in the alphabet. The girls seemed to make the most rapid progress; and two of these—named respectively Rosette and Melvina—could spell words of two syllables, after a tuition of only four weeks.

"Ise glad Ise free now—dat's so!" I one day heard a little curly-headed ebony urchin say to another. They had just been let out of school in Newbern. Struck by the oddity of the saying, I stopped and questioned the lad—

"Why are you glad you're free, my little fellow?"

"'Cause, sar, I can go to school, and learn to read; and den—"

"Well, what then?"

"Why, den de ole woman'll guv me heaps of sweet 'tater pies!"

When the Goldsboro expedition was about to start a requisition for thirty negroes was made upon Mr. Kimball. These, together with a like number from other camps, were to be used as auxiliaries to the pioneer corps. He called them together and stated that an expedition was going off, that Gen. Foster wanted thirty of them to go with it, and called for volunteers. Only six men stepped forward in answer to the call.

"What," said he, "only six! Is that all the men I have?"

When one of the delinquents stepped forward and asked—

"If we goes, Massa Kimball, will dey guv us guns?"

"Yes—you will have guns if you need them."

Upon this announcement they all came forward and offered to go, and he had no easy task to select the thirty men required from the eager crowd.

This was before Wild's brigade had an existence; but showed that the negroes had manhood enough to fight for their freedom —which they have since fully proved on many a bloody field.

---

My task is done—would I could think it well done; but as it is it must go forth, like the ghost of Hamlet's father, with 'all its imperfections on its head.' I might have made it better—but I did not. The world moves on rapidly—things get jumbled up, strangely in these troublous times—and, I suppose, the minds of men get confused and jumbled up also, for sympathy is a law of nature;—life is short, and greater men than I have made mistakes; but no man who fights in the cause of mankind—of universal freedom—can greatly err in its advocacy. The soldier who braves the hardships and perils of the campaign and suffers in a good cause, holds that cause dearer the more he endures for it; and the remembrance of those scenes, filled with glowing and startling pictures, often serves to renew that patriotic fire which forever burns in a corner of his heart. The armies of the rebellion have been flanked—the Confederacy will also soon be flanked, and, like my book, must sooner or later come to an

END.

www.ingramcontent.com/pod-product-compliance
Lightning Source LLC
Chambersburg PA
CBHW021918180426
43199CB00032B/567